Crafting Excellence in Product Management

55 Ways to Help You Be a Good Product Manager

By

Jianchun Xu

Table of Contents

ACKNOWLEDGMENTS

As I set out to write "55 Ways to Help You Be a Good Product Manager," I was acutely aware of the magnitude of the task and the responsibility to provide valuable, actionable insights to those embarking on or navigating through their product management journey. This book is a product of not just my experiences and knowledge, but also the contributions, support, and encouragement from a community of incredible individuals and mentors.

First and foremost, I extend my heartfelt gratitude to my family. Their unwavering support, patience, and belief in my work have been the cornerstone of this endeavor. Their willingness to engage in endless discussions about product management, even when it spilled over into family dinners, speaks volumes of their love and support.

I am deeply thankful to my mentors and colleagues in the product management field. Their rich insights, shared experiences, and willingness to challenge my thinking have been invaluable. Their spirit of mentorship and community embodies the very essence of what makes product management so unique and rewarding.

And finally, to you, the reader, thank you for choosing to embark on this journey with me. Whether you are new to product management or looking to hone your skills, your commitment to learning and growth is commendable. This book is for you, and I hope it serves as a valuable companion in your product management adventure.

Thank you to everyone who played a part in bringing this book to life. Your contributions, big and small, have made this comprehensive guide possible, and for that, I am eternally grateful.

PREFACE

Welcome to "55 Ways to Help You Be a Good Product Manager," a comprehensive guide designed to navigate you through the multifaceted world of product management. Whether you are just starting your journey or looking to enhance your skills, this book is crafted to provide valuable insights, strategies, and real-life examples that will empower you to excel in your role.

Product management is at the heart of successful businesses, driving the creation, development, and delivery of products that meet customer needs and contribute to the company's vision. It is a dynamic and challenging field, requiring a diverse set of skills, a deep understanding of the market, and the ability to lead cross-functional teams. This book is structured to help you master these elements and more, propelling you toward becoming an effective and impactful product manager.

Introduction sets the stage, delving into the significance of product management and outlining the key roles and responsibilities that come with the position. It provides a foundation for understanding the impact a product manager can have within an organization and on the product itself.

Part 1: Fundamental Principles introduces core concepts essential to product management, guiding you through the product lifecycle, customer-centric thinking, and the importance of focusing on problems rather than pre-defined solutions.

Part 2: Research & Understanding Your Market equips you with tools and techniques for gathering valuable user insights, analyzing the competitive landscape, and leveraging data to make informed decisions.

Part 3: Collaborative Skills focuses on the interpersonal aspects of product management, highlighting the importance of effective communication, navigating organizational dynamics, and bridging the gap between different areas of expertise within your team.

Part 4: Roadmapping & Prioritization provides strategies for setting clear objectives, balancing various demands, and ensuring that your product roadmap aligns with both short-term needs and long-term visions.

Part 5: Execution Excellence dives into the practical aspects of product management, offering guidance on writing effective user stories, managing the product backlog, and navigating product launches and iterations.

Part 6: Soft Skills & Personal Growth emphasizes the importance of cultivating emotional intelligence, building resilience, and engaging in continuous learning to enhance your professional development and adaptability in a rapidly changing industry.

Part 7: Customer Engagement & Retention explores strategies for designing compelling user onboarding experiences, driving user engagement, and building lasting relationships with customers.

Part 8: Advanced Product Strategies introduces you to advanced topics such as innovating in saturated markets, managing products on a global scale, and expanding product lines.

Part 9: Leading & Scaling Product Teams provides insights into transitioning from a product manager to a product leader, building and mentoring a high-performing product team, and scaling product operations efficiently.

Part 10: Special Topics covers a variety of relevant issues and emerging trends in product management, including artificial intelligence, remote work, customer co-creation, and navigating regulatory challenges.

Part 11: Preparing for the Future prepares you for future challenges and opportunities, guiding you in predicting and shaping trends, preparing for unexpected market shifts, and adapting to emerging technologies.

Conclusion brings together the themes and lessons from the book, highlighting the ever-evolving nature of the product management role and leaving you with final thoughts to inspire your journey ahead.

"55 Ways to Help You Be a Good Product Manager" is more than just a book; it's a companion in your journey towards becoming a stellar product manager. The strategies, case studies, and insights provided in these pages are aimed at helping you navigate the complexities of product management, enhance your skills, and make a meaningful impact in your organization. Enjoy the journey, embrace the challenges, and strive for excellence in everything you do. Welcome to the world of product management!

Introduction

Welcome to "55 Ways to Help You Be a Good Product Manager." This journey we are about to embark upon is not just about mastering the art and science of product management, but also about unveiling the essence that lies at the core of this exhilarating profession. As we step into this realm, let's first delve into the bedrock of product management – understanding its significance and the pivotal role of a Product Manager.

Why Product Management?

In a world propelled forward by technological innovation, the magic often lies in the marriage of brilliant ideas with meticulous execution. This is where product management takes center stage. It's the unseen force that guides a product from a nascent idea to a market-ready offering, ensuring that the final product not only resonates with customers but also aligns with the strategic vision of the organization.

Product management is not just a function; it's an adventure. It's about solving real-world problems, delighting users, and along the way, discovering the fine balance between creativity, technology, and business acumen. It's a realm where every day brings new challenges, learnings, and the pure joy of seeing your ideas morph into products that make a difference.

The Role and Responsibilities of a Product Manager

Stepping into the shoes of a Product Manager (PM) is akin to being the conductor of a grand orchestra. You are at the helm, orchestrating a harmonious symphony amongst cross-functional teams, aligning them towards a singular vision - the success of the product.

1. **Vision Crafting:**

    - A PM is a visionary, meticulously crafting and nurturing the product's vision, ensuring it aligns seamlessly with the organization's overarching goals.

2. **Strategy Formulation:**

    - It's the PM's forte to chart out the strategic roadmap, setting clear milestones, and ensuring the team is aligned and motivated to march towards them.

3. **Customer Advocate:**

    - PMs are the voice of the customer within the organization, ensuring that the product evolves in sync with the users' needs and desires.

4. **Cross-functional Leadership:**

    - They foster collaboration amongst diverse teams, be it engineering, design, marketing or sales, ensuring seamless communication and a unified focus.

5. **Data-Driven Decision Making:**

    - A PM thrives on data, making informed decisions that drive the product forward, analyzing metrics to continually refine the product strategy.

6. **Continuous Improvement:**

    - The pursuit of excellence is a continuous journey for a PM, always seeking feedback, learning, and iterating to ensure the product is a notch above the rest.

7. **Market Analysis:**

    - Staying attuned to market trends, competitive landscape, and emerging technologies is vital to ensure the product stays relevant and competitive.

8. **Ethical Stewardship:**

    - In a world where technology's impact reverberates across society, a PM also shoulders the responsibility of ethical stewardship, ensuring the product's integrity.

The journey of a Product Manager is as challenging as it is rewarding. It's a role that demands a blend of technical expertise, strategic thinking, and a profound understanding of user needs. As we navigate through the ensuing chapters, we will delve deeper into the myriad facets of product management, equipping you with the knowledge, tools, and insights to excel in your PM journey. So, as you turn the pages, may your passion for product management ignite a trail of innovation, impact, and success.

Part 1: Fundamental Principles

1

Understanding the Product Lifecycle

Every product embarks on a journey from conception to retirement. This journey, often referred to as the Product Lifecycle, is an enthralling narrative of how a product evolves, matures, and eventually, fades into obsolescence. Understanding this lifecycle is akin to having a compass in the bewildering yet exciting wilderness of product management. It provides a structured framework, enabling a Product Manager (PM) to make informed decisions at every juncture. Let's unravel the phases of the Product Lifecycle and explore the quintessence of managing a product through these pivotal stages.

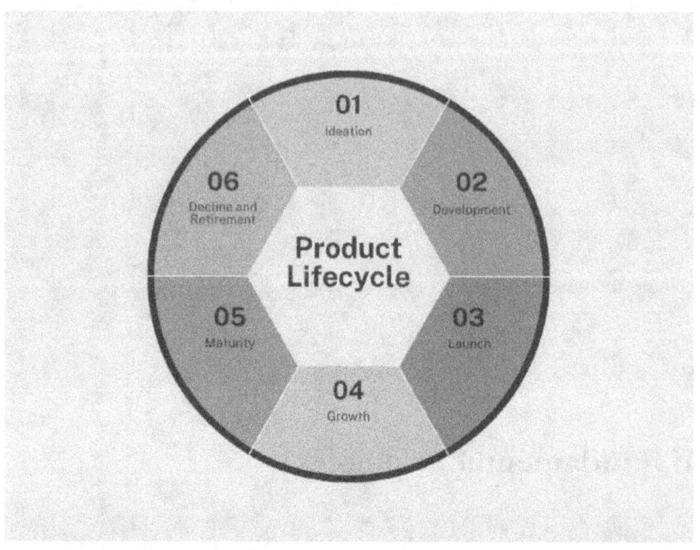

1. **Ideation:**

   - The birth of a product is in the spark of an idea. It's where creativity meets a recognized market need or an unmet desire. During this phase, brainstorming, market research, and customer interviews are your best companions. As a PM, fostering a culture of open ideation, where every voice is heard and every idea valued, can lead to the birth of groundbreaking products.

2. **Development:**

   - Once the idea is crystallized, it's time to roll up the sleeves and delve into the creation. This phase is a bustling hive of activity with cross-functional teams working in unison to transform the idea into a tangible product. A PM plays a pivotal role in ensuring the vision stays intact, the timelines are met, and the resources are optimally utilized.

3. **Launch:**

   - The product launch is the moment of truth. It's when the curtain rises, and the product steps into the spotlight. A meticulously planned launch can catapult a product into the market with a bang. Understanding the market dynamics, crafting a compelling narrative, and ensuring a seamless user experience are the keys to a successful launch.

4. **Growth:**

   - Post-launch, the focus shifts to scaling and expanding the product's market reach. It's about amplifying the user base, enhancing the product features, and exploring new markets. The data gathered from user interactions is gold, helping in refining the product strategy and making data-driven decisions to spur growth.

5. **Maturity:**

   - As the product reaches maturity, the growth may plateau, but the challenge doesn't end. It's about sustaining the momentum, keeping the product relevant amidst evolving market trends, and ensuring a steady revenue stream. Innovations, enhancements, and community engagement are crucial during this phase to keep the product vibrant.

6. **Decline and Retirement:**

   - Every product has a sunset. Recognizing the signs of decline and planning for a graceful retirement is a hallmark of prudent product management. It's about ensuring a smooth transition for users and learning from the journey to imbibe the insights into future endeavors.

7. **Feedback Loops:**

   - Interspersed throughout these phases are feedback loops. They are the nerves of the product lifecycle, conveying the user's pulse and helping in making informed adjustments to the product strategy.

The Product Lifecycle is not just a theoretical framework; it's a lived experience of a product. As a PM, you are the custodian of this journey, ensuring each phase is navigated with foresight, agility, and a profound understanding of the market and user needs. It's about celebrating the highs, learning from the lows, and always keeping the user at the heart of the journey. The ensuing chapters will delve deeper into the intricacies of managing a product through these phases, providing you with the tools, techniques, and insights to excel in your endeavor. As you traverse through the lifecycle of your product, may each phase be a stepping stone to becoming a more insightful, resilient, and successful Product Manager.

2

Embracing Customer-Centric Thinking

The journey of product management is akin to being the captain of a ship sailing through the turbulent yet exhilarating waters of market dynamics, technological innovations, and organizational goals. However, amidst these waves, the lighthouse guiding your voyage is the 'Customer'. Embracing customer-centric thinking is not merely a strategy but a mindset that steers the product towards success. Let's delve into the core essence of customer-centric thinking, unraveling how it shapes a good product manager's ethos.

1. **Understanding Customer Needs:**

    - The bedrock of customer-centric thinking is a deep and nuanced understanding of what the customers need, what they value, and what problems they are facing. Employing techniques like customer interviews, surveys, and user testing can unearth invaluable insights that form the cornerstone of impactful product decisions.

2. **Building Customer Personas:**

    - Crafting detailed customer personas is a powerful way to embody the different user categories your product serves. This exercise not only sharpens the focus but also creates a common understanding among cross-functional teams about who the end users are.

3. **Continuous Engagement:**

    - Customer-centricity is an ongoing dialogue, not a monologue. Establishing channels for continuous feedback and engagement, be it through community forums, social media, or customer advisory boards, keeps the pulse on the customer sentiment and emerging needs.

4. **Co-Creation with Customers:**

- Inviting customers into the product creation process can be a source of groundbreaking innovations. Beta testing, user feedback sessions, and collaborative ideation forums can foster a sense of ownership among customers and yield ideas that may not emerge in a vacuum.

5. **Data-Driven Customer Insights:**

   - In a high-tech world, data is the compass. Leveraging analytics and user behavior data can provide objective insights into how customers are interacting with your product and what can be improved.

6. **Prioritizing Customer Value:**

   - When faced with a plethora of feature requests and enhancement ideas, the compass of customer value can guide in prioritizing the roadmap. Assessing each feature's potential impact on customer satisfaction and value creation can lead to more impactful product decisions.

7. **Designing Intuitive User Experiences:**

   - An intuitive, user-friendly design is the hallmark of a customer-centric product. Investing in UX/UI design and testing with real users can unearth friction points and enhance overall user satisfaction.

8. **Transparent Communication:**

   - Transparency fosters trust. Being open about product updates, addressing concerns promptly, and being honest about product limitations builds a rapport with customers that's invaluable.

9. **Measuring Customer Satisfaction:**

   - Utilizing metrics like Net Promoter Score (NPS) and Customer Satisfaction Score (CSAT) can provide quantitative insights into customer satisfaction, which in turn, can be leveraged to enhance the product.

10. **Cultivating a Customer-Centric Culture:**

- Embedding a customer-centric culture within the team and the broader organization is quintessential. Workshops, training, and regular customer interaction sessions can help in ingraining a customer-centric mindset.

Embarking on the path of customer-centric thinking empowers a product manager to build products that resonate profoundly with the target audience. It's a journey of discovery, empathy, and relentless focus on delivering value that not only meets but exceeds customer expectations. As we traverse through the manifold aspects of product management in the subsequent chapters, let the mantra of customer-centricity be your guiding light, leading you towards creating products that leave a lasting imprint in the market and in the hearts of your customers.

3

Navigating the Business Model Canvas

Introduction

Understanding the Business Model Canvas (BMC) is akin to possessing a compass in the dynamic world of product management. It provides a concise yet comprehensive view of a company's business model on a single page. As product managers, leveraging the BMC can lead to more informed decisions, clearer communication, and a holistic understanding of how products fit within the larger business context.

Deciphering the Business Model Canvas

Originated by Alex Osterwalder, the BMC is a visual chart with nine building blocks detailing a firm's value proposition, infrastructure, customers, and finances. These blocks include Key Partners, Key Activities, Key Resources, Value Propositions, Customer Relationships, Channels, Customer Segments, Cost Structure, and Revenue Streams.

Importance of Each Component

1. **Key Partners:** Who are your essential partners and suppliers? Collaborations can optimize operations and reduce risks.

2. **Key Activities:** What pivotal actions does your business take to function? This could involve production, problem-solving, or platform/network maintenance.

3. **Key Resources:** What assets are critical to your business? This encompasses physical, intellectual, human, and financial resources.

4. **Value Propositions:** What unique value do you offer to customers? This pinpoints the problems you're solving or the needs you're addressing.

5. **Customer Relationships:** How do you interact with your customer segments? This defines the type of relationship a company establishes with specific customer groups.

6. **Channels:** Through which channels do customers want to be reached? This relates to the way a company communicates with and reaches its customer segments.

7. **Customer Segments:** For whom are you creating value? This focuses on the distinct segments of people or organizations an enterprise aims to reach and serve.

8. **Cost Structure:** What are the primary costs tied to your business model? Here, the focus is on understanding the monetary implications of the model.

9. **Revenue Streams:** How does the business generate revenue? This involves identifying the source of money flowing into the business.

Case Study: Spotify's Business Model Canvas

Spotify, a leading music streaming service, effectively utilizes the BMC.

- **Value Proposition:** Unlimited music streaming on-demand.

- **Key Partners:** Record labels, artists, podcast creators.

- **Key Activities:** Platform development, content acquisition.

- **Key Resources:** Music licenses, app development teams.

- **Customer Relationships:** Subscription-based with personalized playlists.

- **Channels:** App on various platforms, partnerships with other tech platforms.

- **Customer Segments:** Free users, premium subscribers, artists.

- **Cost Structure:** Licensing costs, platform maintenance.

- **Revenue Streams:** Advertisements for free users and subscription fees from premium users.

Lesson: Spotify's successful adaptation and navigation of the BMC have enabled it to continuously refine its offerings, address customer needs, and remain a dominant player in the music streaming industry.

Utilizing the BMC in Product Management

For product managers, the BMC isn't just a business tool—it's an essential guide. By aligning product strategies with the BMC, product managers can:

1. **Ensure Alignment:** Products and features can be developed in line with the company's broader objectives.

2. **Identify Gaps:** Spotting missing components or opportunities in the current business model.

3. **Facilitate Communication:** Provides a common language for discussing business models across teams.

Conclusion

The Business Model Canvas is a powerful tool that transforms complex business ideas into understandable, actionable insights. As product managers delve deeper into the intricacies of the BMC, they equip themselves with the ability to navigate their product's journey more effectively, ensuring alignment with broader business objectives and maximizing value for both the company and its customers.

4

Prioritizing Problem-Solving Over Solutions

Introduction

In the vibrant world of product management, it's easy to become enamored with innovative solutions. However, diving headfirst into a solution without deeply understanding the problem it addresses can lead to misaligned products and wasted resources. As product managers, prioritizing problem-solving over solutions ensures that every decision is grounded in genuine user needs and viable market demands.

Understanding the Emphasis on Problem-Solving

At its core, product management is about solving problems for users within the constraints of business. Distinguishing symptoms from root causes, understanding user pain points, and comprehensively analyzing the problem space can illuminate the path to truly impactful solutions.

Why Problem-Solving Matters

1. **User-Centric Approach:** Centering on problems ensures that the focus remains on user needs, enhancing product-market fit.

2. **Resource Optimization:** By deeply understanding the problem, resources are better allocated, minimizing wasted effort on unnecessary features.

3. **Innovation Catalyst:** Often, delving deep into a problem can spark unexpected and innovative solutions.

4. **Stakeholder Alignment:** A clear definition of the problem aligns teams and stakeholders, setting a unified direction.

Case Study: Slack's Evolution

When Stewart Butterfield initially founded Tiny Speck, the objective was to develop a multiplayer online game called 'Glitch'. However, they recognized a distinct problem: communication among the development team was inefficient using available tools.

Instead of pushing forward with 'Glitch', the team shifted focus to the internal communication tool they had built for themselves, which solved a significant problem they faced. This tool later became Slack. By prioritizing the problem of efficient team communication over their initial solution (the game), they created a product now used by millions.

Lesson: Identifying and acting upon a pressing problem can pivot a company towards unforeseen, yet monumental success.

Navigating from Problem to Solution

1. **Problem Validation:** Before seeking solutions, validate that the problem is real, widespread, and worth solving.

2. **User Research:** Engage with users to gain firsthand insights into their challenges and pain points.

3. **Prototyping:** Develop low-fidelity prototypes to test assumptions and gain feedback.

4. **Iterative Testing:** Instead of committing to a full-fledged solution, iterate based on user feedback and adapt as understanding of the problem deepens.

Avoiding Solution-First Pitfalls

1. **Beware of Assumptions:** Rely on data and user feedback rather than making assumptions about what users want.

2. **Stay Agile:** Even after choosing a solution, be ready to pivot if new information emerges about the problem.

3. **Continuous Learning:** Cultivate a learning mindset where understanding problems is an ongoing process.

Conclusion

A successful product manager doesn't just chase after enticing solutions but commits to understanding the intricacies of the problems those solutions intend to address. Prioritizing problem-solving ensures that products remain relevant, impactful, and aligned with both user needs and business objectives. In a world where technology and user behavior are constantly evolving, a foundational emphasis on problem-solving equips product managers with the adaptability and insight needed to drive enduring product success.

Part 2: Research & Understanding Your Market

5

Mastering User Interviews

In the intricate tapestry of product management, user interviews stand out as a potent tool for gaining actionable insights directly from the market. Deep-rooted in empathy, these interviews aim to capture the voice of the customer, unearthing pain points, aspirations, and behaviors that can shape a product's direction.

Understanding User Interviews

User interviews, at their core, are structured conversations where users relay their experiences, preferences, and feedback about a product or a related concept. These discussions are not merely transactional but are rooted in understanding and exploration. Unlike surveys, where responses can be limited and impersonal, interviews allow for depth, nuance, and the discovery of unforeseen insights.

Why Are User Interviews Crucial?

1. **Authentic Feedback**: Engaging directly with users offers raw, unfiltered feedback. This feedback often captures the nuances that quantitative data might overlook.

2. **Empathy Building**: Interviews help product managers understand the user's emotions, motivations, and contexts. This empathy can significantly influence product strategy and design.

3. **Idea Validation**: Before investing heavily in a feature or a new product direction, user interviews can validate (or challenge) initial assumptions.

Conducting Effective User Interviews

1. **Plan Meticulously**: Define the objective of the interview. Is it to understand user behavior, validate a hypothesis, or explore pain points? Knowing your goal can shape the structure of the interview.

2. **Segment Your Users**: Different users might have varied perspectives. Segmenting them based on behavior, demographics, or product usage can provide diverse insights.

3. **Ask Open-ended Questions**: Phrases like "Tell me about…" or "How did you feel when…" encourage detailed responses.

4. **Listen Actively**: The primary goal is to listen. Allow the user to speak freely, and resist the urge to defend or explain the product.

5. **Document Religiously**: Take comprehensive notes or record the conversation (with permission). This documentation is crucial for post-interview analysis.

Case Study: The Transformation of 'TravelX'

TravelX, a budding travel booking platform, was struggling with low user retention. Their interface was sleek, and deals competitive, yet users were not returning after their first booking.

Deciding to tap into the power of user interviews, the product management team set up sessions with both one-time users and regulars. The insights were revealing. New users found the platform's plethora of options overwhelming, often feeling lost amidst the sea of choices.

Acting on this feedback, TravelX introduced a personalized onboarding experience, guiding first-time users through a curated set of choices based on their preferences. This not only made decision-making easier for users but also showcased the platform's commitment to personalized experiences.

The result? A 40% uptick in user retention in the subsequent quarter.

Preparedness for the Unanticipated

Embracing user interviews allows product managers to be agile and responsive. While analytics and market research provide a broad view, interviews can highlight unexpected user behaviors or desires, allowing products to evolve based on genuine user needs.

Moreover, fostering a culture of regular user interaction ensures that products remain user-centric. Regularly scheduled interviews can ensure the product stays aligned with user expectations, evolving market conditions, and emerging user needs.

Closing Thought

Mastering user interviews is more than just a skill—it's an art. It's about cultivating relationships, understanding underlying emotions, and letting user narratives guide product evolution. In the vast universe of product management, the voice of the user, captured through interviews, can be the North Star, guiding decisions, strategies, and innovations.

6

Conducting Competitive Analysis

Introduction

In the dynamic realm of product management, understanding the market landscape is pivotal. Among the crucial steps towards this comprehension is conducting a thorough Competitive Analysis. This process unveils the strengths, weaknesses, opportunities, and threats present in the competitive environment, providing a clear perspective on where the product stands and what it's up against.

The essence of competitive analysis is not about espionage or obsessing over competitors but about understanding the market better. It's a method to view the market through a wider lens, learning from others' successes and failures, and positioning your product strategically amidst the prevailing competition.

Benefits of Conducting Competitive Analysis

1. Strategic Positioning: It aids in carving out a unique value proposition for your product in the market.
2. Informed Decision-Making: It provides insights that lead to better product decisions, reducing uncertainties.
3. Risk Mitigation: Identifying potential threats early can help in formulating strategies to counter them.
4. Opportunity Identification: Spotting gaps in the market or areas where competitors are underperforming can unveil lucrative opportunities.

Case Study:

Netflix's adaptation in its early days: Netflix was a DVD rental service, competing with giants like Blockbuster. Through competitive analysis, they identified the growing trend of online streaming and the declining interest in DVD rentals. This insight led to their pivot towards online streaming, which now defines their identity. Their ability to adapt based on market and competitor analysis has kept them ahead in the fiercely competitive streaming market.

Lesson: A thorough competitive analysis can lead to pivotal insights that not only help in surviving the competition but thriving amidst it.

Steps to Conduct Competitive Analysis

1. Identify Competitors: List down both direct and indirect competitors to get a holistic view.
2. Analyze Competitor Offerings: Understand the features, pricing, and value propositions of competitor products.
3. Market Positioning: Assess how competitors are perceived in the market and how your product compares.

4. Strengths and Weaknesses: Identify the strengths and weaknesses of competitors to find your product's competitive advantage.
5. Customer Reviews and Feedback: Analyze customer reviews of competitors to understand their pain points and satisfaction levels.

Common Pitfalls and How to Avoid Them

1. Overemphasis on Competition: Don't let the competition drive your product strategy entirely. Stay customer-focused.
2. Copying Competitors: Avoid replicating competitor features without understanding if it fits your product's vision and meets your customers' needs.
3. Static Analysis: The market is dynamic; ensure your competitive analysis is an ongoing process, not a one-time activity.

Conclusion

Conducting a comprehensive competitive analysis is a cornerstone for building a product that stands out in the market. It arms product managers with the knowledge needed to make informed decisions, identify unique opportunities, and construct a robust product strategy. In a market teeming with competition, a well-conducted competitive analysis is a linchpin for achieving sustainable product success.

7

Utilizing Market Segment Analysis

Introduction:

In the vast marketplace, not every customer shares the same needs or behaviors. As product managers, our mission is to cater to our users most effectively. Enter Market Segment Analysis—a tool to dissect this vast market into manageable, targeted chunks, each with its unique attributes. Let's unravel its significance and methodology.

1. Grasping the Concept:

- **What is Market Segmentation?**: At its core, market segmentation is the process of dividing a broad market into sub-groups of consumers with shared characteristics, needs, or behaviors.

- **Why is it Crucial?**: By understanding these distinct segments, product managers can tailor offerings, strategies, and marketing communications more effectively, ensuring a higher resonance with potential users.

2. Criteria for Segmenting:

Different products and markets might necessitate different segmentation approaches. Common bases include but are not limited to:

- End Market Segmentation: **Consumer Electronics, Data Centers, Renewable Energy, Industrial, Automotive.**

- Demographic Segmentation: **Age, gender, education, income, etc.**

- Geographic Segmentation: **Region, climate, urban vs. rural.**

- Psychographic Segmentation: **Lifestyle, values, interests.**

- Behavioral Segmentation: **Usage frequency, brand loyalty, spending patterns.**

3. Conducting the Analysis:

- **Research**: Gather data on your current customers and the broader market. This can come from user interviews, surveys, or secondary data sources (e.g. Gartner).

- **Segment Identification**: Based on the criteria chosen, identify the distinct segments within the market.

- **Profile Each Segment**: Dive deeper to understand the characteristics, needs, challenges, and preferences of each segment. Creating detailed personas can be valuable here.

- **Evaluate Segment Attractiveness**: Not every segment holds the same potential. Assess based on size, profitability, accessibility, and alignment with company goals.

4. Translating Analysis into Action:

- **Product Tailoring**: Modify or create features catering to specific segments' needs.

- **Marketing Communication**: Craft messaging that speaks directly to the aspirations or pain points of a segment.

- **Pricing Strategies**: Different segments might have varied price sensitivities. Segment-focused pricing can maximize revenue and adoption.

- **Channel Strategies**: Some segments might be more active online, while others prefer offline channels. Adjust your go-to-market strategy accordingly.

Case Study: Lego's Turnaround through Market Segment Analysis

In the early 2000s, LEGO was facing declining sales and relevance. The company decided to undertake a meticulous market segment analysis to rejuvenate its standing. Through this analysis, LEGO identified several distinct segments within their market, including 'Adult Fans of LEGO' (AFOL) and young creative builders. They realized that while they had been focusing on broadening their appeal, a lucrative segment of adult fans had emerged who cherished complexity and nostalgia. Simultaneously, they recognized the enduring appeal of creative play among young builders.

Acting on these insights, LEGO introduced more complex sets for adult enthusiasts and bolstered their classic colorful blocks range to cater to young imaginative minds. They also tailored their marketing campaigns, showcasing how LEGO is a creative outlet for all ages. This segmentation-led strategy contributed significantly to LEGO's resurgence as a beloved brand across different age groups, showcasing the power of effective market segment analysis in action.

Closing Thoughts:

Market Segment Analysis isn't just a theoretical exercise; it's a strategic roadmap. By understanding the nuances of different market slices, a product manager becomes equipped to make data-driven decisions, ensuring that the product finds its rightful place in the market mosaic.

8

Leveraging Analytics and Data Insights

In the contemporary product management arena, data is a beacon that guides decision-making and strategies. Leveraging analytics and data insights isn't merely about number-crunching; it's about deriving actionable intelligence that propels the product towards market success. This chapter delves into the nuances of leveraging analytics and data insights to enhance understanding, make informed decisions, and optimize product performance.

Grasping the Significance of Analytics

In a world inundated with data, the ability to sift through the noise to obtain meaningful insights is a hallmark of successful product management. Analytics provide a lens to interpret data, understand user behavior, and gauge market trends, which in turn informs strategy and decision-making.

Benefits of Leveraging Data Insights

1. **Informed Decision-Making**: Data insights provide a solid foundation for decisions, reducing ambiguity and guesswork.

2. **Performance Optimization**: Analyzing data aids in identifying areas of improvement, helping optimize product performance.

3. **User Understanding**: It unveils user behaviors, preferences, and pain points, fostering a user-centric approach.

4. **Market Trends Awareness**: Staying abreast of market trends through data analysis helps in adapting strategies timely.

Case Study: Spotify's Data-Driven Persona

Spotify, the global music streaming giant, leverages data insights to enhance user experience continually. By analyzing user behavior and listening trends, Spotify creates personalized playlists and recommendations, significantly enhancing user engagement and satisfaction. Their feature "Discover Weekly," which offers personalized song recommendations, is a testament to the potent synergy of analytics and product management.

Lesson: Harnessing data insights can significantly enhance user experience and engagement, fostering a deeper connection between the product and its users.

Steps to Leverage Analytics and Data Insights

1. **Data Collection**: Implement tools and processes to collect relevant data efficiently.

2. **Data Cleaning and Preparation**: Ensure data integrity by cleaning and preparing data for analysis.

3. **Analytical Tools Utilization**: Employ analytical tools to derive insights from the collected data.

4. **Insight Interpretation**: Translate data insights into actionable strategies and decisions.

5. **Continuous Monitoring**: Establish a system for continuous data monitoring and analysis to adapt to changing dynamics.

Common Challenges and Overcoming Them

1. **Data Overload**: Too much data can be overwhelming. Focus on key metrics that align with your product goals.

2. **Data Accuracy**: Ensure data collection methods are robust to maintain accuracy and reliability.

3. **Skill Gap**: Bridging the skill gap in data analysis within the team through training or hiring experts can be crucial.

Closing Thoughts:

Leveraging analytics and data insights is a cornerstone in modern-day product management. It empowers product managers with the ability to make evidence-based decisions, understand the market and user behavior better, and continuously optimize the product. In a rapidly evolving market, being data-savvy is not just an advantage; it's a necessity. Through a disciplined approach to data analytics, product managers can significantly enhance their product's chances of success in the competitive marketplace.

9

Working with Cross-functional Teams

In the harmonious dance of product development, cross-functional collaboration is akin to choreography. It ensures every department moves with precision, understanding, and alignment, culminating in a product that hits every note perfectly. As a product manager, the onus is on you to ensure that this dance is smooth, synchronized, and, most importantly, effective.

The Imperative of Cross-functional Collaboration

Behind every successful product lies the concerted effort of multiple teams: design, engineering, marketing, sales, and more. These teams, though distinct in function, must operate in unison for the product to achieve its intended goals.

Key Advantages of Cross-Functional Synergy

1. **Holistic Perspective:** Pooling expertise from diverse functions offers a well-rounded view of the product, its challenges, and its potential.

2. **Efficiency in Execution:** Streamlined communication and clear objectives reduce duplication of efforts and save time.

3. **Innovation Boost:** Different teams bring varied problem-solving approaches, leading to innovative solutions.

4. **Stakeholder Engagement:** Teams feel a sense of ownership and commitment when they are actively involved and their input is valued.

Case Study: Airbnb's Seamless Cross-functional Collaboration

Airbnb, the global home-sharing platform, faced a significant challenge in 2014: How to ensure consistency in the user experience across various properties worldwide? The solution lay in the 'Airbnb Host Standards,' a set of guidelines for hosts. However, crafting these standards wasn't the task of a single team.

The product team outlined the user journey. The design team visualized it. The community team, having direct interactions with hosts, provided ground-level feedback, while the engineering team ensured that these standards were seamlessly integrated into the platform. The result? A consistent, high-quality user experience that bolstered Airbnb's reputation and user trust.

Lesson: When teams come together, sharing expertise and insights, they can address complex challenges more effectively and create solutions that resonate deeply with users.

Strategies for Effective Cross-functional Collaboration

1. **Open Communication:** Encourage open dialogues where teams can voice concerns, offer suggestions, and seek clarifications.

2. **Clear Roles & Objectives:** Clearly define the role of each team and the objectives they're aiming for.

3. **Frequent Check-ins:** Hold regular meetings to monitor progress, address roadblocks, and realign if necessary.

4. **Conflict Resolution:** Create mechanisms to resolve disagreements or conflicts constructively and promptly.

5. **Shared Tools:** Use collaborative tools that keep every team on the same page and make project tracking transparent.

Challenges and Solutions in Cross-functional Collaboration

1. **Misaligned Goals:** Establish a shared vision at the start of a project to ensure all teams work towards a common goal.

2. **Communication Breakdown:** Use communication tools, maintain open channels, and schedule regular touchpoints.

3. **Resource Competition:** Clearly outline resource allocation at the project's onset to prevent conflicts.

Closing Thoughts:

Cross-functional collaboration is the bedrock on which great products are built. It's not just about getting different teams to work together, but about creating an environment where they can synergize their expertise for a collective goal. As a product manager, your role is akin to a maestro, orchestrating the beautiful symphony that is product development. And when done right, this collaboration doesn't just create products—it crafts experiences that users cherish.

10

Effective Communication Techniques

In the intricate tapestry of product management, the threads of communication are what bind everything together. An idea, no matter how groundbreaking, can only come to fruition when it's communicated effectively. As a product manager, your role is not only to ideate but also to convey these ideas lucidly to various stakeholders, be it your development team, marketers, or the end-users.

The Power of Clear Communication

In the realm of product management, communication isn't just about transmitting information. It's about ensuring understanding, fostering collaboration, and inspiring action. The ripple effects of clear communication are felt throughout the product lifecycle, from conception to launch and beyond.

Why Communication is Paramount

1. **Transparency:** Clear communication ensures everyone is on the same page, reducing ambiguities and misunderstandings.

2. **Efficiency:** It minimizes back-and-forths, saving precious time and resources.

3. **Stakeholder Engagement:** Effective communication keeps stakeholders informed, involved, and invested in the product's journey.

4. **User Trust:** By communicating product changes, updates, and feedback effectively, trust is built with the end-users.

Case Study: Apple's Mastery in Communication

One of the standout attributes of Apple, beyond its innovative products, is its exceptional prowess in communication. Consider the product launch events Apple conducts. Each product feature is communicated with clarity, backed by its benefits, creating a compelling narrative that captures audience interest. It isn't just about showcasing a product; it's about telling a story.

When Apple removed the headphone jack from the iPhone 7, it could have been a controversial move. However, with effective communication focusing on the vision of a wireless future and the advantages of the lightning port, the transition was smoother than anticipated.

Lesson: Effective communication can not only present features but can also craft narratives that resonate with the audience, making them integral parts of the product journey.

Techniques for Effective Communication

1. **Active Listening:** Pay attention to feedback, concerns, and suggestions from teams and stakeholders.

2. **Simplicity is Key:** Avoid jargon. Use simple language to ensure broad comprehension.

3. **Visual Aids:** Use diagrams, charts, and prototypes to supplement verbal or written communication.

4. **Feedback Loop:** Encourage feedback to ensure your message is understood as intended.

5. **Tailored Communication:** Understand your audience and tailor your message to suit their needs and understanding level.

Barriers to Effective Communication and How to Overcome Them

1. **Information Overload:** Prioritize information. Use summaries and bullet points for clarity.

2. **Cultural Differences:** Be sensitive to cultural nuances. When working with global teams, understanding cultural contexts can aid in clearer communication.

3. **Digital Misunderstandings:** In remote setups, written text can be misconstrued. Use video calls or voice chats when clarity is essential.

Closing Thoughts:

In product management, while features, design, and technology are tangible assets, communication is the intangible thread that binds them all. It's an art and a skill, one that can make the difference between a product's success and stagnation. Cultivating this skill doesn't just amplify your product's potential; it magnifies your impact as a product manager, ensuring ideas don't just remain ideas but translate into impactful realities.

11

Navigating Organizational Politics

The web of human interactions, power dynamics, and vested interests within an organization can often be as intricate as the products you're managing. Navigating organizational politics is an essential skill for product managers. A skill that, when mastered, can accelerate product development, foster collaboration, and even avert potential disasters.

Understanding Organizational Politics

At its core, organizational politics revolves around the use of power and social networking within an organization to achieve changes that benefit the individual or the group. While the term often carries a negative connotation, not all politics are harmful. Understanding this is the first step to navigating them effectively.

Why Navigating Politics Matters

1. **Stakeholder Alignment:** Effective navigation ensures stakeholders are aligned, promoting smoother decision-making.

2. **Resource Allocation:** Politics can influence where resources are directed. By understanding the dynamics, you can better position your product for success.

3. **Conflict Resolution:** Organizational politics often lead to conflicts. Navigating them ensures conflicts are addressed constructively.

4. **Advocacy for Your Product:** In a competitive environment, being politically savvy can help champion your product.

Strategies for Navigating Organizational Politics

1. **Build Strong Relationships:** Foster genuine relationships across departments. Understand their goals and challenges.

2. **Stay Informed:** Keep a pulse on the organization's dynamics. Being aware helps you anticipate challenges and opportunities.

3. **Maintain Transparency:** Be clear about your intentions and actions. This helps in reducing misunderstandings and mistrust.

4. **Choose Your Battles:** Not every political skirmish is worth your energy. Focus on situations that impact your product's success.

5. **Seek Mentorship:** Align with a mentor who understands the organizational landscape and can guide you through complex scenarios.

Challenges in Navigating Politics

1. **Ever-Changing Dynamics:** Organizational landscapes are fluid. New leadership or team structures can shift power dynamics.

2. **Perception Management:** You might be perceived as taking sides. Maintain neutrality and focus on the product's best interests.

3. **Conflict of Interest:** There might be instances where what's best for the product isn't aligned with a powerful stakeholder's vision.

Closing Thoughts:

While product managers often wish to stay removed from politics, the reality is that it's an inherent part of organizational life. Navigating these dynamics gracefully can mean the difference between product success and stagnation. By approaching politics with understanding, strategy, and integrity, product managers can not only survive but thrive in complex organizational landscapes.

12
Bridging the Gap between Technical and Non-Technical Teams

Introduction: The Art of Mediation in Product Management

In the complex ecosystem of product development, product managers often find themselves at the intersection of the technical and non-technical realms. Bridging this gap is crucial, as misunderstandings can lead to misaligned priorities, project delays, and suboptimal outcomes.

Understanding the Dichotomy

The tech team, often comprising developers, QA engineers, and system architects, focuses on feasibility, system constraints, and technical implementations. On the other hand, non-technical teams like sales, marketing, and customer support concentrate on market needs, customer feedback, and go-to-market strategies. The challenge lies in translating the language of code into the language of customer benefits and vice versa.

Strategies for Effective Bridging

1. **Empathy First:** Understand the motivations, challenges, and goals of both sides. Spend a day with a developer or attend a sales pitch to gain firsthand experience.

2. **Clear Documentation:** Create user stories, flow diagrams, and technical specs that are detailed yet easy to understand by all stakeholders.

3. **Regular Check-ins:** Organize frequent cross-functional meetings to ensure everyone is aligned on priorities and understands the progress.

4. **Education & Training:** Host workshops where technical teams explain the basics of their work and non-technical teams share market insights.

5. **Use Common Tools:** Adopt tools that are user-friendly for both technical and non-technical teams to foster collaboration.

The Role of Communication

It's not enough to merely convey messages; it's essential to ensure they're understood. This often means rephrasing technical jargon into layman's terms or turning market feedback into actionable technical tasks.

Case Study: The Feature That Almost Wasn't

A leading e-commerce platform's marketing team found from customer feedback that users wanted a "quick view" feature to see product details without navigating away from the main page. They believed this would enhance the shopping experience and potentially increase sales.

However, when conveyed to the tech team, they were hesitant, citing potential challenges in loading times, database queries, and mobile responsiveness.

The product manager intervened, organizing a joint workshop. The marketing team showcased user testimonials and potential ROI. The tech team, in turn, explained the technical challenges.

Together, they brainstormed a solution: a lightweight "quick view" overlay that pulled minimal data and was optimized for speed. The feature was implemented and became a huge hit, resulting in a 20% increase in user engagement and a noticeable uptick in sales.

Conclusion: The Harmonizing Maestro

A product manager's role is akin to that of a conductor in an orchestra, ensuring that every section plays in harmony. By fostering understanding, open communication, and collaboration between technical and non-technical teams, product managers can ensure that the end product is not only technically sound but also resonates with the market's pulse.

13
Facilitating Productive Meetings

The Symphony of Team Collaboration

Meetings are the crucible where the magic of collaboration happens in product management. When done right, they foster creativity, alignment, and actionable outcomes. However, when mishandled, they can become draining, ineffective, and a mere tick on the calendar. Let's explore the art and science of facilitating productive meetings.

The Core of Productive Meetings

Meetings should serve as platforms for decision-making, brainstorming, or information dissemination. Their efficacy hinges on clarity of purpose, attendee engagement, and actionable outcomes.

- **Type A: Decision-making** - To make decisions on specific issues or challenges.
- **Type B: Brainstorming** - To generate ideas and solutions.
- **Type C: Informational** - To share updates, data, or feedback.

Steps to Ensure Productive Meetings

1. **Clear Agenda:** Establish and communicate the meeting's objective beforehand. A clear agenda provides direction and keeps the discussion on track.

2. **Invite Relevant Stakeholders:** Only involve those whose input is necessary. Overcrowded meetings can lead to diffusion of responsibility and decreased engagement.

3. **Time Management:** Set a strict start and end time. Allocate specific durations for each topic to avoid overruns.

4. **Engage & Facilitate:** Encourage participation, ask open-ended questions, and ensure all voices are heard.

5. **Action Points:** Conclude with clear next steps, responsibilities, and deadlines.

Benefits of Productive Meetings

- **Enhanced Collaboration:** Efficient meetings foster teamwork and collective problem-solving.
- **Time Conservation:** Minimized meeting durations free up time for execution.
- **Clearer Communication:** Well-structured meetings lead to better understanding and fewer misunderstandings.
- **Boosted Morale:** When meetings have tangible outcomes, attendees feel their time was well-spent.

Common Traps and How to Avoid Them

- **No Clear Purpose:** Avoid "meeting for the sake of meeting". Always define the objective.
- **Lack of Preparation:** Send out materials or data beforehand so attendees can come prepared.
- **Dominating Voices:** Ensure that one or two voices don't monopolize the conversation. Actively solicit input from quieter members.
- **Post-meeting Amnesia:** Document minutes, decisions, and action items, and share them promptly.

Case Study: Reviving the Weekly Sync

TechBlitz, a SaaS startup, had weekly product syncs that often ran over time and lacked clear outcomes. Team members began seeing them as obligatory chores.

Upon assuming her role, the new product manager, Maya, decided to revamp the meetings. She implemented a strict 45-minute time cap and introduced a rotating facilitator role. An agenda was sent out two days in advance, and a shared document captured live notes.

Furthermore, Maya introduced a 5-minute "Wins of the Week" segment where team members highlighted their achievements. This not only streamlined the process but also boosted team morale.

The result? The weekly syncs transformed from dreaded calendar events to eagerly anticipated collaborative sessions. Decisions were faster, and team alignment improved significantly.

Conclusion: The Pulse of Effective Collaboration

Facilitating productive meetings isn't just about efficiency; it's about cultivating a culture of respect, collaboration, and mutual growth. For product managers, mastering this skill is not just beneficial—it's imperative. Effective meetings light the path forward, ensuring that every team member is in sync and marching towards a unified goal.

Part 4: Roadmapping & Prioritization

14

Establishing Clear Objectives and Key Results (OKRs)

Introduction: Navigating the Roadmap with Precision

In the voyage of product management, while vision sets the destination, it's the objectives and key results that outline the roadmap. OKRs, a methodology popularized by companies like Google, offer a structured way to set, communicate, and measure objectives. Dive with us into the world of OKRs and learn how they can guide your product to success.

Foundations of OKRs

1. **Objective:** This is a clear, qualitative description of what you aim to achieve. It should be inspiring and easy to remember.

2. **Key Results:** These are specific, quantitative outcomes that, when achieved, signify the objective is met. Ideally, 2-5 KRs are tied to each objective.

Crafting Effective OKRs

1. **Aligned with Vision:** Ensure your OKRs are in sync with the larger product or company vision.

2. **Specific and Measurable:** Key results should be quantifiable and unambiguous.

3. **Attainable yet Ambitious:** While OKRs should push the team, they shouldn't be so out of reach that they demotivate.

4. **Time-Bound:** Set a clear timeframe, typically a quarter, for when the OKRs should be achieved.

5. **Regularly Reviewed:** OKRs aren't "set and forget". Review them regularly to track progress and adjust if needed.

OKRs in Action

1. **Transparency and Alignment:** When everyone knows the OKRs, teams align better and work cohesively towards common goals.

2. **Decision Framework:** OKRs offer a reference point for decision-making, ensuring feature choices or changes align with objectives.

3. **Measurement and Accountability:** With quantitative key results, it's clear if an objective was achieved or missed.

Common Missteps and Their Avoidance

- **Vague Key Results:** Avoid terms like "improve" or "maximize" without specific numbers. Solution? Always quantify the desired outcome.
- **Too Many OKRs:** An overflow of OKRs can dilute focus. Solution? Prioritize and limit the number of OKRs per cycle.
- **Not Adapting:** Sticking to OKRs that are no longer relevant can be detrimental. Solution? Regular reviews and a willingness to pivot when necessary.

The OKR Success Story of RetailRise

When RetailRise, an e-commerce platform, faced stagnating sales, they turned to OKRs. Their primary objective was "Boost User Engagement on the Platform." The attached key results were:

1. Increase daily active users by 20% in Q2.

2. Raise average session duration by 10% by the end of Q2.

3. Achieve a 15% increase in product reviews and ratings by Q2 end.

With these OKRs in place, the product team rolled out features enhancing user experience, while the marketing team initiated campaigns to drive reviews. By the end of Q2, RetailRise not only met but exceeded all key results, marking a triumphant comeback.

Final Takeaway

Establishing clear OKRs is akin to setting up signposts on your product journey. They provide direction, maintain alignment, and ensure that everyone is rowing in harmony towards a shared horizon. By mastering the art of OKRs, product managers can lead with clarity, purpose, and measurable impact.

15

Mastering the Art of Prioritization

Sifting Through the Noise: The Quest for What Truly Matters

In the intricate dance of product management, prioritization is a step that often distinguishes success from mediocrity. Amidst a sea of demands, expectations, and opportunities, discerning what truly deserves your attention is both an art and a science. Journey with us as we unlock the secrets of effective prioritization.

Principles of Pragmatic Prioritization

1. **Align with Vision:** Every prioritization decision should be a step closer to the overarching product or company vision.

2. **Value vs. Effort:** Assess tasks based on the value they bring and the effort they demand. High value and low effort tasks usually take precedence.

3. **Stakeholder Input:** Involve key stakeholders in the prioritization process to gather diverse perspectives and foster buy-in.

4. **Flexibility:** The landscape can change rapidly. Be ready to adjust priorities as new information or situations arise.

5. **Limit Work in Progress:** Focus delivers results. Instead of juggling many tasks, prioritize a few and execute them well.

Frameworks for Focused Prioritization

1. **MoSCoW Method:** Classify tasks into Must have, Should have, Could have, and Won't have.

2. **RICE:** Score tasks based on Reach, Impact, Confidence, and Effort.

3. **Kano Model:** Prioritize features based on how they influence customer satisfaction.

4. **Cost of Delay:** Evaluate tasks based on the potential cost of postponing them.

Pitfalls of Poor Prioritization

1. **Spreading Too Thin:** Without clear priorities, teams can become overwhelmed, leading to mediocre execution across tasks.

2. **Lost Opportunities:** Failing to prioritize might mean missing out on high-impact opportunities.

3. **Stakeholder Dissatisfaction:** When everything seems important, stakeholders might feel their concerns are overlooked.

The TechStart Prioritization Pivot

TechStart, a budding SaaS company, was struggling to retain users. Their product had numerous features, but user engagement was waning. The product team felt constant pressure to deliver new features, believing variety would enhance retention.

However, an analysis revealed that while they had many features, only a few were frequently used and valued. Taking a bold step, TechStart prioritized refining and enhancing these core features over adding new ones.

The result? A more focused product that resonated with users. Engagement metrics improved, and churn rates decreased. TechStart's decision to prioritize depth over breadth was a game-changer.

In Summation

Prioritization isn't just about ticking off tasks on a list; it's about ensuring that every tick counts. It's the compass that ensures every step taken is purposeful and aligned with the desired destination. By honing the skill of prioritization, product managers can ensure that they, their teams, and their products consistently move in the right direction.

16
Balancing Short-Term and Long-Term Goals

Walking the Tightrope: The Delicate Balance of Now and Tomorrow

Charting a product's journey is akin to navigating a ship through ever-changing waters. While it's vital to address the immediate obstacles, one must never lose sight of the distant shore. As product managers, the challenge lies in harmonizing immediate needs with future aspirations. Let's delve into the delicate equilibrium of balancing short-term actions with long-term visions.

Strategies to Strike the Right Balance

1. **Clear Vision and Mission:** Always keep the product's ultimate vision in focus. While short-term goals should address immediate challenges or opportunities, they must align with the larger mission.

2. **Iterative Planning:** Embrace agile methodologies. They allow for a series of short-term actions that cumulatively build towards long-term objectives.

3. **Feedback Loops:** Regularly solicit feedback from stakeholders. This ensures that both short-term tasks and long-term strategies remain relevant and value-driven.

4. **Resource Allocation:** Dedicate resources to both immediate tasks and foundational work that propels long-term goals.

5. **Regular Review:** Consistently evaluate the relevance of long-term goals in the face of changing market conditions or internal dynamics.

Benefits of a Balanced Approach

1. **Resilience:** A dual focus ensures that while the product adapts to immediate market feedback, it remains steadfast in its larger objectives.

2. **Stakeholder Engagement:** By showing progress in the short term while communicating the long-term vision, stakeholders remain engaged and invested.

3. **Optimized Resource Utilization:** Resources aren't stretched thin over immediate fires but are methodically allocated for sustained growth.

Challenges and How to Overcome Them

- **Myopic Vision:** An overemphasis on short-term goals can divert from the ultimate objective. *Solution?* Regular alignment workshops to refocus on the broader vision.

- **Procrastination on Future Goals:** Deeming long-term objectives as distant can lead to complacency. *Solution?* Break down long-term goals into actionable yearly or quarterly milestones.

- **Resource Crunch:** Sometimes, immediate needs can consume all available resources, leaving none for the future. *Solution?* A dedicated innovation or foundational team that focuses on long-term objectives.

GreenTech's Evolutionary Leap

GreenTech, a startup dedicated to sustainable solutions, had developed an eco-friendly product with vast potential. However, market education and immediate adoption were challenges. They were torn between refining the product for the distant future or pushing for immediate sales.

Choosing a balanced path, GreenTech initiated short-term campaigns to drive awareness and seed the market, while a dedicated team worked on next-generation improvements. Their iterative releases ensured that early adopters benefitted from continuous improvements, and their long-term vision materialized as the market matured and recognized the product's value.

In three years, not only did GreenTech become a market leader, but they also pioneered standards in sustainability, their ultimate vision.

Final Thoughts

In the world of product management, balancing the urgency of the present with the promises of the future is a continual act. It's not about choosing one over the other but orchestrating them in harmony. When done right, short-term wins become stepping stones to long-term triumphs.

17
Addressing Technical Debt

The Invisible Weight: Unearthing the Burden

Much like financial debt, technical debt accrues over time, often silently, weighing down products and hindering progress. Failing to address it timely can lead to larger repercussions. As product managers, understanding, measuring, and addressing technical debt is vital for ensuring a product's health and adaptability. Let's dissect the nuances of technical debt.

Strategies for Managing Technical Debt

1. **Regular Audits:** Conduct systematic reviews and quality assurance checks to identify potential hotspots of technical debt.

2. **Prioritization:** Not all debts need immediate attention. Classify them based on their impact and the effort required to address them.

3. **Documentation:** Ensure all quick fixes, workarounds, or compromises are well-documented to make future resolutions easier.

4. **Stakeholder Education:** Make non-technical stakeholders aware of the importance of addressing technical debt to secure their buy-in for dedicating resources.

Consequences of Ignoring Technical Debt

1. **Reduced Agility:** High technical debt can make it challenging to implement new features or make changes.

2. **Performance Issues:** Over time, unresolved debts can lead to sluggish performance or even system crashes.

3. **Increased Costs:** Longer the delay in addressing the debt, the more resources it might consume in the future.

4. **Team Morale:** Continually working on projects riddled with technical debt, whether in hardware or software, can demoralize the development team.

TechWise's Rejuvenation

TechWise, a SaaS company, had been in the market for over a decade. With changing technologies and multiple hands touching the code, the platform had accumulated significant technical debt. As competitors launched newer, agile products, TechWise started losing its market share.

Sarah, the new Product Manager, recognized the urgency to address this looming debt. She initiated a tech-debt audit, categorizing issues based on severity and impact. While she faced resistance to pause new feature development, Sarah illustrated the long-term gains of a rejuvenated platform.

She set up dedicated "debt-reduction" sprints, interwoven with regular feature sprints. Developers were empowered to refactor and improve the codebase. Within a year, the platform was not only faster and more reliable but also more adaptable to new feature integrations.

TechWise not only regained its lost market share but also increased its customer satisfaction significantly.

In Retrospect

Technical debt isn't merely a development challenge; it's a product challenge. A proactive approach to understanding, communicating, and addressing this debt ensures that the product remains healthy, agile, and competitive. As with financial debts, the key lies in recognizing, addressing timely, and ensuring prudent decisions to prevent unnecessary accumulation.

18

Aligning Stakeholder Expectations

The Delicate Dance: Navigating Varying Visions

One of the intricate aspects of product management is not just dealing with product intricacies but managing the various stakeholders involved. Each stakeholder, be it marketing, sales, development, or executives, comes with unique perspectives and priorities. Aligning these varied expectations into a cohesive product vision is both an art and a science. Dive with us as we unravel this delicate dance of alignment.

Strategies for Aligning Stakeholder Expectations

1. **Open Communication:** Establish a routine of transparent communication. Regularly update stakeholders about product status, challenges, and roadmaps.

2. **Feedback Loops:** Create systematic channels for stakeholders to voice their concerns, feedback, or insights about the product.

3. **Shared Vision:** Ensure every stakeholder understands the broader product and company vision. This helps in aligning individual priorities towards a unified goal.

4. **Decision Frameworks:** Use clear criteria or frameworks when making decisions, ensuring stakeholders understand the rationale behind product choices.

5. **Stakeholder Workshops:** Organize collaborative sessions where stakeholders can brainstorm, discuss, and align on product direction.

Potential Misalignments and Bridging Gaps

1. **Differing Priorities:** Sales might prioritize features that help close deals, while developers might focus on technical robustness.

Solution? Educate each team about the other's priorities and find a balanced approach.

2. **Timeline Mismatches:** Marketing might want a feature launched for an upcoming campaign, while development sees it as a longer-term project. Solution? Regular roadmapping sessions to sync timelines.

3. **Resource Conflicts:** Multiple departments vying for the same resources. Solution? Clear product roadmaps and resource allocation based on company-wide priorities.

Sailing Smoothly: The Story of TrendTech

TrendTech, a growing tech firm, faced a challenge. The marketing team felt sidelined, believing their inputs on product features were constantly overlooked. On the other hand, the development team felt overwhelmed by ad-hoc feature requests.

Mia, an experienced Product Manager. She began by organizing a series of workshops, bringing together teams from marketing, sales, development, and customer support. Mia facilitated discussions where each team outlined their priorities and challenges.

She then introduced a prioritization framework, ensuring that any feature request or change was evaluated based on customer value, business impact, and technical feasibility. Mia also set up a bi-weekly product update meeting, where each team was updated about product progress, upcoming features, and rationale behind decisions.

Over time, not only did the teams feel more aligned, but the product itself began to resonate better with customers, as it was shaped by holistic insights from all departments.

In Reflection

Stakeholder alignment isn't about pleasing everyone; it's about ensuring everyone is moving in the same direction, even if their paths differ. Through clear communication, collaboration, and a shared vision, product managers can navigate the maze of stakeholder expectations, ensuring a product that's not just technically sound but also resonates with the market and fulfills business goals. It's a dance that, when choreographed well, results in a harmonious and impactful performance.

Part 5: Execution Excellence

19

Writing Effective User Stories

The Art of Storytelling: Crafting a Clear Narrative

Like an author delicately weaving a plot, a product manager crafts user stories to bridge the gap between user needs and technical implementation. This narrative, while concise, encapsulates the essence of what the user requires. Dive into the realm of user story creation and its pivotal role in product management.

Strategies for Writing User Stories

1. **INVEST Principle**: Remember the acronym 'INVEST' - Independent, Negotiable, Valuable, Estimatable, Small, Testable. Each user story should embody these traits.

2. **User-Centricity**: Begin with "As a [type of user], I want to [action] so that [benefit/rationale]."

3. **Acceptance Criteria**: Clearly define the conditions that must be met for the story to be deemed complete.

4. **Avoid Technical Jargon**: Ensure your story is comprehensible to all, not just the technically-inclined.

5. **Feedback Loop**: Constantly gather feedback on your stories to refine them further. Collaborate with both the technical team and stakeholders.

Incorporating Context and Clarity

1. **Visual Aids**: Use diagrams or mock-ups to provide a clearer picture of your vision.

2. **User Journeys**: Position the story within the larger user journey to showcase its significance and interrelation with other features.

Common Pitfalls and Their Remedies

- **Vagueness**: Ambiguous user stories can confuse development team. Solution? Be as specific as possible without making the story too lengthy.
- **Assuming Knowledge**: Believing everyone knows the context. Solution? Always provide necessary background, even if it seems repetitive.
- **Over-Complication**: Unnecessarily long and intricate stories. Solution? Break them down into smaller, manageable stories.

Crafting the Story for 'ShopEase'

Jenna, the product manager for an e-commerce platform, realized that their checkout process was cumbersome. She could have vaguely asked the team to "improve the checkout process." Instead, she wrote: "As a shopper, I want a single-page checkout so that I can complete my purchase faster and with ease." The development team, with this clear directive, revamped the checkout page, streamlining the user flow and reducing drop-offs. Sales increased, and user reviews praised the simplified process.

In Conclusion

Writing an effective user story is both an art and a science. It demands empathy towards the user, a clear understanding of the product, and an ability to communicate concisely. When done right, it acts as a guiding star for the development team, ensuring the final product truly resonates with its users. Remember, in the realm of product management, a well-told story can shape the success trajectory of your product.

20

Managing the Product Backlog

The Living Repository: The Pulse of Your Product

Think of the product backlog as the beating heart of your product management endeavors. This dynamic collection of tasks, features, and enhancements propels your product forward. Just like a gardener tends to their garden, a product manager should nurture their backlog. Delve into the world of backlog management to ensure product health and progress.

Guidelines for a Flourishing Product Backlog

1. **Clear Articulation**: Every item in the backlog should be distinct and understandable, reducing ambiguity for developers and stakeholders.

2. **Prioritize Relentlessly**: Continuously rank items based on value to the user, business impact, and technical feasibility.

3. **Regularly Refine**: The backlog is not static. It needs frequent grooming to remove outdated items, adjust priorities, or split large items.

4. **Categorize Items**: Use tags or labels to categorize items (e.g., bugs, features, enhancements) to aid in clarity and organization.

5. **Define Acceptance Criteria**: For every item, detail the conditions that should be met for it to be considered complete.

Balancing Act: Short-Term Needs vs. Long-Term Vision

1. **Iteration Focus**: While it's essential to prioritize tasks for the upcoming sprint or release, always keep an eye on the long-term product vision.

2. **Feedback Incorporation**: Use customer and stakeholder feedback to reprioritize or introduce new items, ensuring the product remains user-centric.

Common Roadblocks and Navigation Strategies

- **Backlog Bloat**: A backlog that becomes too vast to manage. Solution? Regularly schedule backlog grooming sessions to declutter and reprioritize.
- **Over-Prioritization**: Every item seems like a top priority. Solution? Use objective criteria or scoring systems to rank items genuinely.
- **Stakeholder Conflicts**: Different stakeholders might push for their items. Solution? Maintain transparent communication and explain prioritization decisions.

The Tale of 'ConnectHub'

Elena, the product manager for a social networking platform 'ConnectHub', faced an overwhelming backlog with hundreds of items. With stakeholders demanding their features and the development team seeking clarity, chaos ensued.

Deciding to regain control, Elena organized a series of backlog refinement workshops. Stakeholders were invited, and together they redefined priorities, eliminated redundancies, and aligned on the immediate and future goals. By visualizing the backlog using a priority matrix, Elena ensured that both strategic objectives and urgent needs were balanced.

Within months, 'ConnectHub' saw a faster release cycle, with features more aligned with user needs. Stakeholder satisfaction soared as they witnessed their concerns being addressed systematically.

In Conclusion

A well-managed product backlog is pivotal for product success. It offers clarity, direction, and focus to the entire product team. By ensuring it's always prioritized, organized, and aligned with the product's goals, a product manager paves the way for smooth execution and delivery. Remember, a product's excellence often reflects the health of its backlog.

21

Ensuring Quality Assurance Best Practices

Beyond Testing

Quality assurance (QA) is more than just finding bugs—it's about ensuring a seamless and delightful user experience. It's the difference between creating a product that works and one that resonates. Navigate the meticulous world of QA and understand why it's the unsung hero of product excellence.

Strategies for Effective Quality Assurance

1. **Holistic Test Planning**: Develop comprehensive test plans covering functional, performance, security, and usability aspects of the product.

2. **Automate Intelligently**: While manual testing has its place, automation can boost efficiency. Prioritize repetitive and regression tests for automation.

3. **Continual Feedback Loop**: Ensure that QA teams have a direct line to development team for quick issue resolution and iterative testing.

4. **Environment Simulation**: Test products in environments that closely replicate real-world user scenarios, across devices and platforms.

5. **User-centric Testing**: Beyond technical tests, incorporate user acceptance testing (UAT) to gauge real-world usability.

QA Synergy with Product Management

1. **Early Engagement**: Involve QA teams from the ideation phase. Their feedback can preempt potential challenges.

2. **Shared Understanding**: Ensure that QA understands not just the product's functionalities but also its goals and user personas.

Challenges and Proactive Measures

- **Ever-changing Product Features**: Constant product updates can disrupt testing. Solution? Modular test plans that can adapt without full rewrites.

- **Incomplete Bug Reports**: Vague bug reports can hinder resolutions. Solution? Standardized bug report templates and training for clarity.

- **Time Constraints**: Sometimes, testing might be rushed due to deadlines. Solution? Prioritize critical test cases and ensure at least those are comprehensively checked.

The Chronicle of 'FinSave'

Alex was the product manager for 'FinSave', a financial tracking app. Post-launch, user reviews highlighted numerous glitches, tarnishing its market reputation. Alex recognized that while the product had been tested, the QA practices had gaps.

Revamping the QA approach, he ensured that the QA team was included from the design phase. This early involvement highlighted potential pitfalls, reducing post-development errors. Alex also pushed for environment simulations, revealing device-specific issues previously overlooked.

Automation was introduced, making regression testing quicker and more efficient. User-centric testing was emphasized, with real-world scenarios and user personas driving the QA process. The transformation was evident. Subsequent versions of 'FinSave' received glowing reviews, with users appreciating the bug-free experience.

In a turning point, a user commented, "Feels like the team behind 'FinSave' truly understands what we need. It just works!" Alex realized that their newfound success wasn't just about fixing bugs—it was about refining user experience.

In Conclusion

Quality assurance is the intricate dance between technology and user experience. It's about proactive problem-solving, foresight, and a deep understanding of user needs. As product managers, championing robust QA practices can be the differentiator between a good product and a great one. After all, in the world of products, perfection lies in the details.

22

Navigating Product Launches

From Conception to Launchpad: The Symphony of a Successful Debut

Launching a product is the crescendo of countless hours of work, a harmonized effort that culminates in presenting your creation to the world. Like a spacecraft's launch, meticulous preparation ensures soaring success rather than a fiery fiasco. Dive into the art of launching your product the right way.

Strategies for a Smooth Product Launch

1. **Integrated Go-to-Market Strategy**: Harmonize your marketing, sales, and product strategies to ensure a unified message and approach.

2. **Beta Testing**: Engage early adopters or a select group of users to gather preliminary feedback and make adjustments before the grand release.

3. **Launch Phasing**: Consider a phased approach, releasing the product to certain markets or user segments first to manage risk and gather insights.

4. **Cross-functional Collaboration**: Foster close collaboration between departments—sales, marketing, tech support—to ensure all teams are aligned and prepared.

5. **Post-Launch Monitoring**: Continuously monitor user feedback, product performance, and sales metrics post-launch to quickly address any arising issues.

Anticipating and Mitigating Risks

1. **Detailed Launch Plan**: Have a documented plan detailing every aspect of the launch, including roles, timelines, and contingencies.

2. **Resource Redundancy**: Ensure backup resources—whether it's server capacity for a software product or extra inventory for a physical product.

3. **Crisis Communication Plan**: Be prepared with a communication strategy in case of unforeseen hiccups during the launch.

Challenges and Proactive Measures

- **Mismatched Expectations**: The market might not perceive the product's value as you do. Solution? Robust market research and clear messaging.
- **Technical Glitches**: A product might face unforeseen technical issues. Solution? Comprehensive pre-launch testing and a dedicated tech support team on standby.

Chronicle of 'EcoVessel'

Jordan was spearheading the launch of 'EcoVessel', a sustainable water purification solution. Market anticipation was high. However, during the initial product demos, several technical glitches cropped up, risking the product's reputation even before its official debut.

Jordan and her team decided to delay the launch. They engaged in rigorous beta testing, identifying not just the technical issues but also fine-tuning the product based on user feedback. Simultaneously, the marketing team tweaked their strategies based on insights from the beta testers.

The revised launch was not just glitch-free but also saw higher engagement, with users appreciating the product improvements. A potential disaster was turned into a resounding success, with 'EcoVessel' becoming a market leader within months.

The experience reinforced Jordan's belief in thorough preparation, adaptability, and the value of listening to users.

In Conclusion

Navigating a product launch is akin to steering a ship through stormy seas into the tranquil harbor. It requires foresight, preparation, and adaptability. While challenges are inevitable, a well-prepared product manager can transform these into opportunities, ensuring not just a successful launch but a product that truly resonates with its audience.

23

Handling Product Iterations and Feedback Loops

The Circle of Continuous Improvement: Bridging Gaps One Loop at a Time

Product development is never truly linear nor finalized. It's a spiral, constantly turning back on itself for refinement. A product's true success isn't just in its launch but in its evolution, steered by feedback loops. Let's delve into the dynamic world of product iterations.

Strategies for Effective Feedback Integration

1. **Feedback Collection Mechanisms**: Employ tools like surveys, user interviews, and in-app feedback prompts to gather insights directly from users.

2. **Categorization and Prioritization**: Group feedback into themes or categories and prioritize them based on factors like user impact, feasibility, and alignment with the product vision.

3. **Rapid Prototyping**: Convert feedback into tangible prototypes. This allows for a clearer understanding and facilitates further user testing.

4. **Iterative Development Cycles**: Adopt agile methodologies, allowing regular and frequent updates to the product based on feedback.

5. **Feedback Loop Closure**: Always circle back to users who provided feedback, updating them on changes made or explaining why certain suggestions weren't implemented.

Maximizing Value from Feedback

1. **Diverse Feedback Channels**: Ensure feedback comes from varied user segments to avoid biases or skewed perspectives.

2. **Feedback Analysis**: Use analytics tools to identify patterns or correlations in feedback, helping in making data-driven decisions.

3. **Internal Feedback**: Don't overlook feedback from internal teams like sales, support, and marketing. They often offer valuable frontline insights.

Challenges in Iterative Development and Solutions

- **Overwhelm by Volume**: Large volumes of feedback can be daunting. Solution? Automated feedback processing tools and clear categorization strategies.
- **Conflicting Feedback**: Different users might have contrasting opinions. Solution? A/B testing to objectively evaluate multiple suggestions.
- **Avoiding Feature Creep**: Constant iterations can lead to unnecessary features. Solution? Stay aligned with the core product vision and user personas.

Chronicle of 'NoteMaster'

Jake helmed 'NoteMaster', a note-taking app. Post-launch, feedback poured in, ranging from UI improvements to new feature requests. Jake realized that while some suggestions were valuable, others could derail the product from its core focus.

Instead of rushing into iterations, Jake's team categorized the feedback and mapped it against their product vision. They prototyped the most aligned suggestions and tested them with a user group. Some features, like collaborative note-making, were a hit, while others were dropped.

Additionally, they found that many users weren't aware of existing features, prompting an improved onboarding process. By the next update, 'NoteMaster' had not just addressed its shortcomings but also enhanced its strengths.

The experience solidified Jake's belief in feedback not just as a problem pointer but also as a path illuminator.

In Conclusion

Handling product iterations and feedback loops is the art of listening, discerning, and acting. It's about keeping the product alive, relevant, and ever-improving. The iterative cycle can be as challenging as it is rewarding, but a well-navigated feedback loop can transform a good product into a great one.

Part 6: Soft Skills & Personal Growth
24
Cultivating Emotional Intelligence

The Symphony of Emotions: Tuning In To Inner Harmonies

Product management is not just about managing products, but also managing relationships, expectations, and, sometimes, conflicts. Navigating this complex human landscape requires a tool more potent than any software: Emotional Intelligence (EI). Dive in as we explore how cultivating EI can make you a stellar product manager.

Components and Strategies for Enhancing Emotional Intelligence

1. **Self-Awareness**: Recognize your emotions and their impact. Maintain a journal or practice reflection to understand emotional triggers and patterns.

2. **Self-Regulation**: Manage disruptive emotions and impulses. Techniques like deep breathing, timeouts, and constructive self-talk can be useful.

3. **Motivation**: Nurture your passion and enthusiasm. Set clear goals, celebrate milestones, and constantly reconnect with your product's vision.

4. **Empathy**: Understand the emotions of others. Practice active listening, ask open-ended questions, and imagine yourself in others' shoes.

5. **Social Skills**: Build healthy relationships. Engage in team-building activities, provide constructive feedback, and nurture a culture of open communication.

Emotional Intelligence in Action

1. **Conflict Resolution**: Use empathy to understand conflicting viewpoints, ensuring everyone feels heard.

2. **Stakeholder Management**: Tailor your communication based on the emotions and motivations of different stakeholders.

3. **User-Centricity**: Truly empathize with user pain points, leading to more intuitive product solutions.

Challenges and Their Solutions

- **Overwhelm by Emotions**: Being in touch with emotions can sometimes be overwhelming. Solution? Seek mentorship or counseling and set aside regular 'me-time' for emotional well-being.
- **Misreading Emotions**: Incorrectly gauging someone's emotions can lead to miscommunication. Solution? Clarify by asking, rather than assuming, and invest time in building deeper connections.
- **Balancing Logic and Emotion**: Product decisions should be a blend of emotion and logic. Solution? Use data-backed decisions complemented by empathy-driven insights.

The Chronicles of Maya, the Emotionally Intelligent PM

Maya was overseeing a crucial product feature launch. However, team morale was low due to a recent project setback. Instead of pushing her team harder, Maya, sensing the emotional undercurrents, arranged a feedback session.

During this session, team members shared their concerns and frustrations. Using her emotional intelligence, Maya not only acknowledged their feelings but also worked with them to co-create a plan to move forward. She also incorporated regular emotional check-ins into team meetings.

Months later, not only was the feature successfully launched, but the team also felt more cohesive and empowered. Maya's emotional intelligence had transformed a challenging phase into a growth opportunity for the team.

In Conclusion

Emotional Intelligence isn't just about being sensitive; it's about leveraging emotions—both yours and others'—as a strategic resource. In the world of product management, where human interactions are central, cultivating EI can make the difference between a good product manager and a great one. Embrace the symphony of emotions, and watch as it orchestrates success in your product journey.

25

Building Resilience and Handling Failure

The Phoenix Principle: Rising Stronger

Failure is an inevitable part of any journey, and product management is no exception. However, the mark of a truly exceptional product manager is not the ability to avoid failure, but the capacity to rise from it stronger and wiser. Let's delve into how building resilience can turn setbacks into springboards.

Strategies for Cultivating Resilience

1. **Embrace a Growth Mindset**: View challenges as opportunities to learn and grow. Remember, abilities can be developed.

2. **Maintain a Strong Support Network**: Cultivate relationships with mentors, colleagues, and friends who can provide guidance and encouragement.

3. **Develop Emotional Intelligence**: Understand and manage your emotions, especially in times of stress.

4. **Practice Mindfulness and Self-Care**: Engage in activities that promote well-being and reduce stress.

5. **Learn from Failure**: Analyze what went wrong, identify lessons learned, and apply them to future projects.

Resilience in the Face of Failure

1. **Post-Mortem Analysis**: After a failure, conduct a thorough review to understand what happened and why.

2. **Foster a Safe Environment for Failure**: Encourage a culture where failure is seen as a learning opportunity, not a cause for punishment.

3. **Celebrate Small Wins**: Recognize and celebrate progress and achievements, no matter how small.

Challenges and Their Solutions

- **Fear of Failure**: This can paralyze and prevent taking necessary risks. Solution? Foster a culture that embraces risk and sees failure as a stepping stone to innovation.
- **Burnout**: Continuous stress and failure can lead to burnout. Solution? Ensure there is a balance between work and life, and practice regular self-care.
- **Lack of Perspective**: In the moment, failure can seem insurmountable. Solution? Take a step back, look at the bigger picture, and understand this is just a bump in the road.

Case Study: Sandra's Steadfast Comeback

Sandra, a product manager at a tech startup, was overseeing the development of a new app. Despite her best efforts, the app received negative reviews upon launch due to unforeseen technical glitches.

Instead of succumbing to despair, Sandra channeled her frustration into determination. She rallied her team, conducted a comprehensive post-mortem analysis, and identified the key areas that needed improvement. She also made it a point to maintain open communication with her users, assuring them that their concerns were being addressed.

Within months, the app was relaunched with significant improvements, resulting in positive user feedback and increased downloads. Sandra's resilience had not just saved the product, but also transformed a potential career setback into a testament to her leadership and tenacity.

In Conclusion

Building resilience is not about becoming impervious to failure, but about learning to navigate it with grace and strength. As a product manager, your journey will undoubtedly be fraught with challenges. However, by cultivating resilience, you ensure that you are not defined by your setbacks, but by your ability to overcome them and emerge stronger on the other side. Remember, in the crucible of failure, the resilient product manager is forged.

26

Time Management for Busy Product Managers

Mastering the Clock: A Symphony of Efficiency

As a product manager, you are the maestro of your product's symphony, coordinating different sections to create a harmonious performance. But what happens when the tempo increases, and the pieces become complex? The key is masterful time management. Let's delve into strategies to maximize productivity while maintaining balance.

Strategies for Effective Time Management

1. **Task Prioritization**: Identify and focus on high-impact activities. Utilize frameworks like Eisenhower Matrix to categorize tasks based on urgency and importance.

2. **Time Blocking**: Dedicate specific time blocks for different activities. This minimizes multitasking and enhances focus.

3. **Leverage Productivity Tools**: Utilize tools like Trello or Asana for task management, and Calendly for scheduling.

4. **Set SMART Goals**: Ensure your objectives are Specific, Measurable, Achievable, Relevant, and Time-bound.

5. **Practice the Two-Minute Rule**: If a task takes less than two minutes, do it immediately. This reduces backlog and keeps your to-do list manageable.

Efficiency in Action

1. **Delegate Effectively**: Understand your team's strengths and delegate tasks accordingly. This ensures tasks are completed efficiently and helps in team development.

2. **Minimize Distractions**: Create a workspace that minimizes distractions.

3. **Take Breaks**: Incorporate short breaks into your schedule to prevent burnout and maintain high performance.

Challenges and Their Solutions

- **Overcommitment**: Taking on too much can lead to burnout. Solution? Learn to say no and set realistic expectations.
- **Procrastination**: Delaying tasks can lead to last-minute rushes. Solution? Break tasks into smaller, manageable parts and start immediately.
- **Lack of Focus**: Constant interruptions can hinder productivity. Solution? Set specific times for checking emails and messages, and communicate your focus periods to your team.

Case Study: Alex's Turnaround

Alex, a senior product manager at a growing tech firm, found himself constantly overwhelmed, juggling multiple products and responsibilities. His productivity was waning, and burnout was imminent.

Realizing the need for change, Alex decided to overhaul his approach to time management. He started with task prioritization, focusing on activities that drove the most value. He implemented time blocking, dedicating specific periods for deep work, meetings, and administrative tasks.

He also made conscious efforts to minimize distractions and started using productivity tools to keep track of tasks and deadlines. Within months, Alex experienced a significant boost in productivity and job satisfaction, turning what seemed like an insurmountable challenge into a manageable and enjoyable routine.

In Conclusion

Effective time management is not about doing more in less time; it's about doing the right things at the right time. For a product manager juggling a plethora of tasks, mastering this skill is imperative. By prioritizing tasks, leveraging productivity tools, and minimizing distractions, you can turn time into your ally, ensuring that every moment counts towards achieving your product's symphony of success. Remember, time is the one resource we can't renew, so use it wisely, and watch as your productivity and job satisfaction soar.

27

Staying Updated with Industry Trends

Navigating the Waves of Change: A Continuous Learning Journey

In the ever-evolving world of technology and business, staying stagnant is equivalent to moving backward. For a product manager, being in sync with the latest industry trends is not just beneficial; it's imperative. This section will guide you through strategies to keep yourself updated and case studies illustrating the tangible impact of staying informed.

Proactive Learning Strategies

1. **Subscribe to Industry Newsletters and Blogs**: Follow authoritative sources and thought leaders in your industry. Newsletters like CB Insights, TechCrunch, and specific industry blogs can be a goldmine of information.

2. **Participate in Online Forums and Communities**: Platforms like Reddit, LinkedIn, and Product Management specific forums are great for discussions, knowledge sharing, and staying abreast of the latest trends.

3. **Attend Conferences and Webinars**: Events are not just for networking; they are also an opportunity to learn from experts and gain insights into emerging trends.

4. **Engage with Academic and Research Publications**: Stay connected with academia to understand theoretical advancements that could translate into industry innovations.

5. **Leverage Social Media**: Follow industry hashtags, join relevant groups, and engage with content to ensure your feed is a source of continual learning.

Applying Knowledge to Practice

1. **Incorporate Learnings into Your Product Strategy**: Use your newfound knowledge to innovate and improve your product strategy.

2. **Share Knowledge with Your Team**: Cultivate a culture of learning within your team. Share articles, discuss trends during meetings, and encourage others to stay informed.

3. **Experiment and Innovate**: Don't be afraid to experiment with new technologies or strategies within your product. This could be through A/B testing or pilot programs.

Challenges and Their Solutions

- **Information Overload**: With the abundance of sources, it's easy to feel overwhelmed. **Solution?** Curate your sources, focus on quality over quantity, and allocate specific times for reading.
- **Applying Knowledge**: Simply knowing the trends is not enough; applying them is key. **Solution?** Set aside time for strategic planning and experimentation.
- **Keeping Up with the Pace**: The speed at which industries evolve can be daunting. **Solution?** Focus on continuous learning and remain adaptable.

Case Study: Transforming Traditional Retail

Emily, a product manager at a traditional retail chain, realized the pressing need for digital transformation in her industry. She proactively started attending webinars, subscribed to relevant newsletters, and engaged with e-commerce communities.

Her efforts paid off when she stumbled upon an emerging trend in augmented reality (AR) for virtual try-ons. Recognizing its potential, she proposed an AR-based app allowing customers to try products virtually.

The project was a success, leading to increased online engagement, higher conversion rates, and setting the company apart from competitors. Emily's initiative to stay updated and her ability to apply her learnings not only benefited the company but also established her as an innovative leader.

In Conclusion

Staying updated with industry trends is a continuous journey of curiosity, learning, and application. By embracing this journey, you not only enhance your own skills but also contribute significantly to your product's success and your team's development. Remember, the world is constantly changing, and your ability to navigate these changes with informed confidence will define your journey in product management.

28

Continuous Learning and Professional Development

Fostering a Growth Mindset: The Key to Evolving Excellence

The landscape of product management is continually evolving, rendering lifelong learning not just an asset but a necessity for any product manager aiming for excellence. This section dives into the importance of continuous learning, strategies to enhance your professional development, and case studies highlighting the transformative power of an unwavering commitment to growth.

Strategies for Constant Growth

1. **Set Clear Learning Goals**: Establish what you want to achieve in your learning journey. Whether it's mastering a new tool, understanding a specific market, or developing leadership skills, having clear objectives keeps you focused.

2. **Leverage Online Learning Platforms**: Platforms like Udemy, and LinkedIn Learning offer a plethora of courses tailored to product management and associated skills.

3. **Join Professional Networks and Associations**: Engaging with professional associations provides access to resources, mentorship, and networking opportunities.

4. **Seek Feedback and Mentorship**: Regularly seek feedback on your performance and areas of improvement. Find a mentor who can guide you through your career, offering insights and advice.

5. **Embrace Cross-Functional Learning**: Don't limit your learning to product management alone. Understanding the nuances of marketing, sales, design, and engineering can make you a more well-rounded professional.

Applying Learning to Real-World Scenarios

1. **Practice What You Learn**: Apply new knowledge and skills to your current role, ensuring that your learning translates to tangible improvements in your work.

2. **Share Your Knowledge**: Teach others what you've learned. This not only reinforces your own understanding but also contributes to the growth of your team.

3. **Stay Curious and Question Everything**: Cultivate a mindset of curiosity. Question existing processes and always look for ways to improve.

Challenges and Their Solutions

- **Finding Time for Learning**: With the demands of a product management role, finding time for learning can be challenging. **Solution?** Schedule regular, dedicated time for learning.
- **Translating Learning to Practice**: Acquiring knowledge is one thing; applying it is another. **Solution?** Set actionable goals and seek opportunities to implement your learnings in real-world scenarios.
- **Keeping Momentum**: It's easy to start strong and lose momentum over time. **Solution?** Set achievable, short-term goals and celebrate milestones along the way.

Case Study: Elevating E-commerce Excellence

Michael, a product manager in a burgeoning e-commerce company, realized the potential of artificial intelligence (AI) in enhancing customer experience. Determined to leverage this trend, he embarked on a learning journey, taking up online courses on AI and machine learning.

He didn't stop there. Michael applied his newfound knowledge to enhance the company's product recommendation engine, resulting in a 20% increase in customer engagement and a significant boost in sales.

His proactive approach to learning and application not only yielded tangible results for his company but also established him as a thought leader in his domain, paving the way for further career progression.

In Conclusion

Continuous learning and professional development are the hallmarks of a successful product manager. By embracing a growth mindset, actively seeking learning opportunities, and applying your knowledge to real-world challenges, you ensure that you are always at the forefront of your field, ready to lead your product to new heights. Remember, the journey of learning never ends, but each step forward is a step towards excellence.

Part 7: Customer Engagement & Retention

29

Designing User Onboarding Flows

As a product manager, you've poured your heart into creating a product that meets your users' needs. However, the journey doesn't end there. How your users engage with your product for the very first time can set the tone for their entire experience. This is where designing an effective user onboarding flow comes into play.

The First Steps into a New World

Imagine inviting someone to your home for the first time. Do you let them fumble in the dark, or do you guide them, show them where the light switch is, offer them a drink, and make them feel at ease? User onboarding is that warm, illuminating welcome for your product users.

For both hardware and software products:

- **Hardware:** Think of a new electronic device. A quick start guide can help users understand its primary functions, ensuring they can use it straight out of the box without feeling overwhelmed.

- **Software:** Consider a new app download. Guided tooltips, intro videos, or step-by-step walkthroughs can help users understand the core features, enabling them to derive immediate value.

Design Principles for Effective Onboarding

1. **Simplicity is Key:** Your users shouldn't feel overwhelmed. Break down the onboarding process into easily digestible steps, introducing one core feature at a time.

2. **Immediate Value:** Show users the most valuable aspect of your product as soon as possible. Let them experience that "Aha!" moment early on.

3. **Feedback Loops:** Use progress bars or checklists to let users know how far they've come and what's left. This instills a sense of accomplishment.

4. **Personalization:** If possible, tailor the onboarding experience based on user preferences. A personal touch can make the experience feel unique.

Mistakes to Avoid

- **Overloading Information:** Avoid bombarding users with too many details. Focus on what's crucial for them to get started.

- **Forgetting Mobile Users:** Ensure that your onboarding flow is optimized for mobile devices if you have a digital product.

- **Skipping User Feedback:** Regularly gather feedback on your onboarding process and iterate based on real user experiences.

Closing Thoughts

An effective onboarding process can be the difference between a user who stays engaged and one who abandons your product. As you shape this journey, always place yourself in the user's shoes and ask, "Does this help them understand and love the product as I do?" Your answer will guide you towards creating an unforgettable first impression.

30

Strategies for User Engagement

In the vast world of product management, creating an exceptional product is merely the beginning. To ensure success, continuous user engagement is vital. Think of it as nurturing a relationship; it requires understanding, consistency, and evolving with time.

The Parable of the Town Festival

Imagine a quaint town that hosts an annual festival. The first year, there's curiosity, and a good number of townsfolk attend. The organizers pull out all the stops, and it's a grand success. But what happens the next year? If it's the same old attractions, many might give it a miss. However, if there are new events, interactive sessions, and evolving experiences, the festival not only retains its attendees but also attracts new ones. Similarly, for your product to thrive, you must constantly innovate and engage.

Core Strategies for User Engagement

1. **Feedback is Gold:** Regularly solicit feedback. Understanding user needs, grievances, and suggestions can be instrumental in keeping your product relevant and continuously improving.

2. **Content as a Hook:** Regularly update content, be it blog posts, tutorials, webinars, or user guides. Fresh content can bring users back and reinforce the value of your product.

3. **Gamification:** Introduce elements of fun and competition. Leaderboards, badges, or rewards can incentivize users to engage more frequently.

4. **Personalized Experiences:** Leverage user data to tailor experiences. A user is more likely to engage if the product feels like it's made "just for them".

5. **Regular Updates:** Consistently roll out updates, new features, or improvements. It not only addresses issues but also reiterates your commitment to providing value.

6. **Community Building:** Create forums, user groups, or social media communities where users can interact, share experiences, and form a bond over your product.

Mistakes to Sidestep

- **Being too Pushy:** While reminders are good, avoid overwhelming users with too many notifications or emails.

- **Neglecting User Concerns:** Always address issues promptly. An unresolved problem can lead to a user disengaging permanently.

- **Static Strategies:** The digital world evolves rapidly. What worked a year ago might not be effective now. Always be ready to adapt.

In Conclusion

Engaging users is an ongoing journey, one that requires attentiveness and proactivity. Always remember, the goal is not just to get a user to try your product but to make them fall in love with it, time and time again. Like any flourishing relationship, it's the sustained effort that makes all the difference.

31

Handling Customer Feedback and Complaints

In the dynamic landscape of product management, customer feedback is the North Star. While positive feedback propels us forward, negative feedback, if handled correctly, can pave the path to unparalleled growth. Embracing feedback, both good and bad, is instrumental in crafting a product that stands the test of time.

The Tale of the Unsatisfied Baker

In a bustling town, Amelia opened a bakery, pouring her heart into every delicacy she crafted. Customers flocked, and reviews were generally positive. But one day, a customer complained about a stale cake. Instead of dismissing it, Amelia invited the customer for a chat over tea. She listened, apologized, and offered a fresh cake on the house. More importantly, she delved deep, improving her storage techniques to ensure it never happened again. News of her gracious handling spread, and her business flourished like never before.

This parable underscores a fundamental truth: negative feedback is an opportunity in disguise.

Guidelines for Managing Feedback and Complaints

1. **Listen Actively:** Ensure the user feels heard. Avoid getting defensive; instead, genuinely understand their point of view.

2. **Acknowledge and Apologize:** A simple acknowledgment can diffuse a lot of tension. Even if the issue isn't directly your fault, apologize for the inconvenience caused.

3. **Act Promptly:** Addressing concerns swiftly is paramount. Even if a complete solution takes time, keep the user updated about the steps you're taking.

4. **Learn and Iterate:** Use feedback as a tool to improve. Analyze recurring complaints and proactively resolve underlying issues.

5. **Feedback Channels:** Make it easy for users to provide feedback. Be it through surveys, feedback forms, or direct communications, ensure users have multiple avenues to reach out.

6. **Celebrate Positive Feedback:** While it's essential to address negative feedback, cherishing the positive ones boosts team morale and showcases what's working.

Mistakes to Avoid

- **Generic Responses:** Avoid canned, impersonal responses. Each user's concern is unique, and your reply should reflect that.

- **Delay in Communication:** A timely response can make the difference between a retained customer and a lost one.

- **Ignoring Silent Feedback:** Not all users vocalize their concerns. Monitor user behavior, drop-off rates, and other metrics to capture implicit feedback.

In Conclusion

Feedback, especially complaints, is a treasure trove of insights. It offers a direct line into users' minds, highlighting what you're doing right and where you can improve. In the realm of product management, a complaint handled well can turn a disgruntled user into a brand ambassador. Remember, it's not about avoiding mistakes but about how you rise after making one. Embrace feedback, and let it guide your journey to excellence.

32

Advocating for the User Experience (UX)

Every product tells a story, and the narrative's success hinges largely on the user experience (UX). UX is not just about design; it encapsulates the entire journey a user undertakes, from the first interaction to becoming a loyal advocate. As a product manager, being a staunch advocate for a stellar UX is pivotal.

The Fable of the Labyrinthine Library

In the heart of a vibrant city, a grand library was erected. With vast collections, it was a treasure trove for avid readers. However, visitors often complained about the confusing layout, hard-to-reach books, and an absence of guidance.

Then, came a librarian, Maya. She put herself in the shoes of the visitors, journeyed through the maze-like aisles, and experienced the challenges firsthand. Driven by the desire to optimize the experience, she reorganized the sections, introduced signages, and trained guides. Visitors now spent hours lost in books rather than the labyrinth. The library transformed from being a grand structure to a cherished sanctuary for readers.

This tale accentuates the undeniable value of a well-crafted user experience.

Steps to Advocate for UX

1. **Empathize with Users:** Begin with understanding the user journey. Use personas, journey maps, and empathy sessions to truly comprehend user pain points and aspirations.

2. **Gather Data:** Utilize analytics, heatmaps, and feedback to gather quantitative and qualitative insights about how users interact with your product.

3. **Collaborate with UX Teams:** Establish a strong partnership with UX designers and researchers. Attend design reviews, participate in usability testing, and ensure a two-way communication channel.

4. **Prioritize User-Centric Features:** In product roadmaps, prioritize features enhancing UX. Remember, even a fantastic feature, if not user-friendly, can hinder product success.

5. **Educate Stakeholders:** Regularly communicate the importance of UX to stakeholders. Use data to highlight how good UX positively impacts business metrics.

6. **Iterate Based on Feedback:** UX is not static. Continuously gather feedback and be ready to pivot or refine the user experience.

Common Challenges

- **Balancing Business Goals and UX:** At times, there might be a tug-of-war between immediate business goals and long-term UX benefits. Advocating requires striking the right balance.

- **Overcoming Resistance:** Not all stakeholders might understand the nuances of UX. It's crucial to be patient, educate, and bring them aboard.

The Ultimate Payoff

Remember, in the vast sea of products, the ones that resonate with users, addressing not just their needs but also their unspoken desires, truly stand out. As a product manager, let advocating for UX be your compass, guiding your product to unparalleled success.

33

Building Brand Loyalty and Trust

At the heart of every successful brand lies a strong foundation of trust and unwavering loyalty from its customers. These elements aren't built overnight but are cultivated through consistent delivery, genuine connections, and understanding customers' intrinsic values. As a product manager, instilling trust and fostering brand loyalty is integral to sustainable growth.

The Legend of the Ever-Full Inn

Nestled at the edge of a bustling town stood the Ever-Full Inn, always brimming with patrons. Its competitors were grander, with more luxurious amenities. Yet, travelers, merchants, and townsfolk always chose the Ever-Full Inn.

The secret? The innkeeper, Eldric. He remembered names, stories, and even the favorite dishes of his guests. The Inn might not have had lavish suites, but it promised a warm meal, a listening ear, and consistent service. Over time, the inn wasn't just a place to rest but became a home away from home for many. This unwavering loyalty was built on trust, consistency, and genuine connection.

Blueprint to Building Brand Loyalty and Trust

1. **Consistency is Key:** Deliver consistent product quality and service. Ensure that every interaction reaffirms the brand's promise, just like Eldric's reliable service at the Ever-Full Inn.

2. **Open Channels of Communication:** Listen actively to your customers. Feedback, whether praise or criticism, is invaluable. Address concerns promptly and openly.

3. **Deliver Genuine Value:** Beyond the core offering, how does your product enrich your customers' lives? Perhaps it saves them time,

brings joy, or alleviates a pain point. Always aim to deliver that extra ounce of value.

4. **Engage Authentically:** In today's digital age, authentic engagement goes a long way. Whether it's through social media, community forums, or personalized emails, ensure your brand communicates genuinely.

5. **Reward Loyalty:** Consider loyalty programs, exclusive previews, or special offers for long-standing customers. Show appreciation for their continued patronage.

6. **Educate and Empower:** Equip your customers with knowledge. Offer webinars, write blogs, or provide resources that help them make the most of your product.

Challenges on the Path

- **Changing Market Dynamics:** With ever-evolving market trends and competition, staying top-of-mind for customers can be challenging. Continuous innovation and adaptation are vital.

- **Managing Negative Feedback:** Negative feedback or public criticism can dent trust. However, addressing it transparently and genuinely can turn detractors into promoters.

The Endgame

Brand loyalty and trust translate into repeat business, positive word-of-mouth, and a buffer against market fluctuations. While acquiring new customers is essential, retaining existing ones is often more cost-effective and rewarding.

Like the Ever-Full Inn, your product might be one among many. Still, with trust and loyalty, it can be the first choice for many. As you navigate the product management landscape, let these two pillars guide your strategies, decisions, and interactions. Let it be the adhesive that binds your brand to its customers.

Part 8: Advanced Product Strategies

34
Innovating in Saturated Markets

The bustling marketplace is a vast sea. Sometimes, these waters turn red from fierce competition, with every brand vying for a piece of the pie. How, then, does one innovate and discover fresh, blue oceans in such saturated markets?

The Tale of The Revolutionary Cobbler

In a town filled with cobblers, Samuel had a dilemma. Each cobbler offered almost identical shoes, and competition was cutthroat. Instead of battling on pricing or design, Samuel pondered a different approach.

One day, he introduced shoes with removable soles, allowing wearers to switch them out based on terrain or preference. This innovation wasn't just about shoes anymore—it was about adaptability and personalization.

Samuel found his blue ocean, and customers flocked to his store, seeking not just shoes, but an experience.

Strategies for Innovating in Saturated Markets

1. **Rethink Customer Needs:** Dive deeper into customer feedback and latent needs. Like Samuel, seek gaps that competitors have overlooked.

2. **Disruptive Innovation:** Introduce products that differ significantly from the norm. They might cater to a smaller audience initially, but they can open up new market segments.

3. **Augment User Experience:** Sometimes, the product remains the same, but the way it's delivered or experienced undergoes a transformation. Think about Apple's retail stores, which revolutionized tech shopping experiences.

4. **Submarket Targeting:** Even in saturated markets, there might be niche segments that are underserved. Cater specifically to these submarkets.

5. **Collaborative Partnerships:** Collaborate with other businesses to co-create value. This could be cross-promotion, bundle offers, or entirely new product creations.

6. **Elevate Brand Storytelling:** Shift from selling a product to selling an emotion or a story. Powerful narratives can set a brand apart even in crowded spaces.

Challenges to Anticipate

- **Initial Resistance:** Any deviation from the norm might face resistance. Early adopters will be few, but their feedback will be gold.

- **Replication by Competitors:** Once you find success, competitors will attempt to replicate. Hence, continuous innovation and brand strengthening become crucial.

- **High Initial Costs:** R&D for innovation in established markets might require substantial investments.

In Conclusion

Finding blue oceans in red seas is a challenge that demands creativity, deep customer understanding, and a willingness to take calculated risks. But when achieved, the rewards—both in terms of brand differentiation and financial returns—are immense.

Remember Samuel. When every cobbler was looking at leather and laces, he saw an opportunity in soles. It's a lesson for all product managers: Innovation isn't just about being different; it's about being better in ways that truly matter to the customer.

35

Navigating Global Product Management

The world is now an intricate tapestry of interconnected markets, each with its own challenges, opportunities, and quirks. Global product management isn't just about scaling a product—it's about adapting, understanding, and resonating with diverse cultures, economies, and ecosystems.

The Chronicles of Maya, the Global Product Manager

Maya had always been adept at managing her tech product in her home country. But when the decision came to expand globally, she was met with a mosaic of unexpected challenges. From understanding European data privacy laws to decoding the digital behaviors in Southeast Asia, every region presented a new puzzle.

Yet, with each challenge, Maya learned invaluable lessons that transformed her approach to product management.

Strategies for Navigating Global Product Management

1. **Localized Research:** Before diving into a new market, immerse yourself in its culture, behaviors, and nuances. What works in one region might flop in another.

2. **Regulatory Understanding:** Every region comes with its regulatory maze. Whether it's GDPR in Europe or the Great Firewall in China, a global product manager must be attuned to these guidelines.

3. **Localized User Experience:** From language to UI/UX design, products need to resonate with local sentiments. Maya realized that color perceptions, for example, varied greatly between Western and Eastern cultures.

4. **Global Team Collaboration:** Building diverse teams from various regions ensures insights from those who understand local cultures

best. Regular sync-ups, clear communication, and mutual respect are pillars of such collaboration.

5. **Pricing Strategy Adjustments:** Economic disparities mean a one-size-fits-all pricing might not work. Understand purchasing power and set prices accordingly.

6. **Feedback Mechanisms:** Establish channels where users from different regions can voice their feedback. Their insights can be markedly different from what you're used to.

Challenges to Brace For

- **Cultural Missteps:** Even the best intentions can lead to cultural faux pas. Always be ready to learn and apologize if necessary.

- **Logistical Delays:** Whether it's setting up servers or shipping physical products, global operations can face logistical challenges.

- **Varying Growth Rates:** Some markets might adopt your product rapidly, while others take time. Patience and persistence are vital.

In Conclusion

For Maya, the journey of global product management was akin to sailing turbulent seas, but it also came with the thrill of discovering new horizons. With each market, she became not just a better product manager but also a global citizen, understanding the ties that bind us and the uniqueness that defines us.

For those venturing into global product management, remember that the world might be diverse, but at the heart of every market is a human, with aspirations, needs, and emotions. Resonate with them, and you resonate globally.

36
Addressing Ethical Considerations in Product Design

Introduction: The Ethical Fabric of Innovation

In the modern, technologically-advanced era, it's tempting to get swept up by the allure of groundbreaking innovations. However, for product managers, it's crucial to remember that innovation is not just about advancements; it's also about responsibility. Every product decision has the potential to impact millions, making ethics an imperative component in product design.

The Underlying Ethical Dilemmas

While technology has revolutionized the way we function, it has also presented a host of ethical concerns:

1. **Surveillance and Privacy**: As smart devices become ubiquitous, there's an increasing risk of violating user privacy. How do product managers ensure that innovations respect individual rights?

2. **Algorithmic Biases**: Machine learning and AI, though powerful, can often mirror and perpetuate societal biases. How do product teams prevent these biases from affecting their users?

3. **Digital Well-being**: With the world becoming more connected, the lines between digital and real-life interactions blur. How do product managers ensure their tools don't lead to digital addiction?

Strategies for Ethical Product Design

1. Empathetic Design Thinking: Begin by understanding your users deeply. Utilize empathetic design thinking to foresee potential harm and design with the user's best interest at heart.

2. Transparent Communication: Always be upfront about how a product works, especially when it comes to user data. Clear communication builds trust.

3. Diverse Product Teams: Diverse teams bring a wide range of perspectives, which can be instrumental in identifying potential ethical pitfalls.

4. Ethical Audits: Regularly review and assess your product against ethical standards. This could be done in-house or by third-party experts.

5. User Feedback Loop: Encourage users to voice ethical concerns. Their on-ground feedback can provide valuable insights that might be overlooked internally.

Case Study: The Ethical Navigation of a Fitness App

A fitness application was designed to motivate users by ranking them based on their activity levels. Initial tests indicated high engagement. However, some users felt demotivated when consistently ranked lower, leading to feelings of inadequacy.

The product team had an ethical dilemma: while the feature increased engagement (a business win), it had potential mental health implications for a segment of its users.

The resolution? The app introduced personalized milestones, allowing users to compete against their records, shifting the focus from competition with others to self-improvement. The result was a win-win: high engagement and a positive user experience.

Final Thoughts

Ethical considerations in product design are about striking the right balance between business objectives and moral responsibility. As product managers, the choices we make shape the societal implications of innovations. The goal should always be to create products that enhance lives, without compromising values or well-being. By addressing ethical considerations head-on, we not only protect users but also ensure the longevity and credibility of our products in an increasingly conscious market.

37

Harnessing the Power of A/B Testing

Introduction: The Science Behind Decision Making

When it comes to product management, gut feelings are valuable but can sometimes lead us astray. Enter A/B testing, a systematic approach that lets real user data guide our product decisions. By splitting user groups and testing variant features, product managers can ascertain what truly resonates with their audience.

The Essence of A/B Testing

A/B testing, often called split testing, involves comparing two versions of a webpage, app, or other product feature to determine which performs better in terms of a specific goal, be it click-through rates, conversions, or user retention.

- **Version A**: The control - the current version of your product/feature.

- **Version B**: The variant - the new version you think might be better.

Steps to Effective A/B Testing

1. **Set Clear Objectives**: Know what you're trying to achieve. Whether it's increased user engagement, higher conversion rates, or improved user satisfaction, your objective should be clear and measurable.

2. **Choose Your Variables**: Decide on the specific elements you want to test. It could be a new feature, a different color scheme, or even a reworded call-to-action.

3. **Randomize Your Sample**: Ensure that you're dividing your user base randomly to avoid any selection bias.

4. **Gather & Analyze Data**: Use analytics tools to gather data on how each group interacts with the respective version. After sufficient data has been collected, analyze the results.

5. **Implement Changes**: If Version B (the variant) outperforms Version A (the control), consider implementing the changes. If not, you've gained valuable insights without disrupting your user base.

Benefits of A/B Testing

- **Data-driven Decisions**: Move from intuition-based choices to decisions grounded in real user data.

- **Reduced Risks**: Test new features or changes without fully committing, reducing the potential negative impact.

- **Optimized User Experience**: Continuously refine and improve your product based on what resonates most with users.

- **Increased ROI**: By understanding what drives conversions or engagement, product managers can optimize for maximum return on investment.

Pitfalls to Avoid

- **Testing Too Many Variables**: If you change multiple elements at once, it's hard to pinpoint which one caused the change in user behavior.

- **Not Giving the Test Enough Time**: A/B tests need to run long enough to collect meaningful data.

- **Ignoring External Factors**: Be aware of external events that could skew results, like a holiday sale or a viral social media post.

Case Study: Streamlining a Subscription Process

A music streaming app noticed that many users abandoned the subscription process midway. To address this, they hypothesized that the multi-page sign-up was too lengthy.

They designed an A/B test where:

- **Version A (Control)**: Retained the original multi-page subscription process.

- **Version B (Variant)**: Introduced a single-page, streamlined subscription process.

After running the test for a month, Version B showed a 15% higher conversion rate. The product team then implemented this streamlined process, leading to increased subscriptions and reduced drop-offs.

Final Thoughts

A/B testing is a powerful tool in a product manager's arsenal, allowing them to fine-tune their products based on empirical evidence. However, its success hinges on methodical planning, clear objectives, and astute interpretation of results. By regularly employing A/B testing, product managers can continuously evolve their products to better serve their users, driving both user satisfaction and business success.

38

Expanding Product Lines and Diversification

Introduction: Beyond the Singular Offering

The journey of a product doesn't conclude with its successful launch. A mature product may represent an opportunity for growth beyond its initial scope. Here lies the strategy of product line expansion and diversification – an essential move for businesses wishing to capture a larger market share, reduce risks, and harness new revenue streams.

Defining Product Line Expansion & Diversification

Product Line Expansion: It refers to adding more products to an existing product line to capture a broader audience. For instance, a company selling herbal teas might introduce new flavors or variants targeting different health benefits.

Diversification: A strategy to introduce new products in new markets. It is riskier than line expansion as it requires entering an unfamiliar market with an unfamiliar product.

Why Consider Expansion and Diversification?

- **Meeting Diverse Customer Needs**: Different consumers have varying needs. An expanded product line caters to a broader audience.

- **Risk Management**: Diversifying offerings can shield a company from downturns in one particular segment.

- **Capitalizing on Brand Equity**: Leverage the trust and recognition built around the brand to introduce new offerings.

- **Tapping into New Revenue Channels**: Multiple products mean multiple revenue streams.

Steps for Effective Expansion & Diversification

1. **Market Research**: Understand the market's unmet needs. Are there gaps your product can fill? Can your brand enter a new sector?

2. **Leverage Existing Assets**: Utilize existing resources, technology, or infrastructure for the new offering, ensuring cost-effectiveness.

3. **Assess Financial Implications**: Determine the costs associated and predict potential returns.

4. **Test and Iterate**: Before a full-scale launch, test the new product on a smaller audience to gauge response and refine accordingly.

Pitfalls to Beware

- **Overextension**: Expanding too quickly can strain resources and dilute brand identity.

- **Neglecting Core Products**: In the race to diversify, don't forget what made your brand successful in the first place.

- **Entering Overcrowded Markets**: Without a unique value proposition, the new product might struggle in a saturated market.

Final Words

Product line expansion and diversification are strategic levers that can propel a brand to new heights. However, it's a game of calculated risks. With thorough market insights, a strong understanding of one's capabilities, and a relentless focus on delivering value, product managers can navigate this complex terrain, turning potential pitfalls into avenues for unprecedented growth.

Part 9: Leading & Scaling Product Teams

39
Growing From a Product Manager to a Product Leader

The Evolutionary Path: The Journey of Becoming

Every product manager dreams of the day when their skills, expertise, and leadership are recognized. This day marks the transition from being a product manager to a product leader. However, the journey involves more than just a title change. It is a transformation in mindset, responsibilities, and the broader impact one has on the organization and the product itself.

Understanding the Distinction

Before we delve deeper, let's understand the fundamental differences between a product manager and a product leader:

- **Scope of Influence**: While a product manager might be responsible for specific features or products, a product leader oversees multiple products or entire product lines, guiding the strategic direction.

- **Depth of Execution**: A product manager often immerses themselves in day-to-day tasks, user stories, and backlogs. In contrast, a product leader must elevate their vision, focusing on long-term strategies, team dynamics, and organizational alignment.

- **Stakeholder Management**: Product leaders engage more with executives, influencing company strategy and ensuring product vision aligns with business goals.

Key Steps to Transition

1. **Develop a Visionary Outlook**: Start seeing the bigger picture. Understand market trends, organizational goals, and how your product fits within this vast ecosystem.

2. **Enhance Soft Skills**: Leadership is about inspiring and motivating. Work on your communication, conflict resolution, and team-building skills.

3. **Engage with Executives**: Build relationships with higher-ups, understanding their vision, and aligning your strategies accordingly.

4. **Mentor & Coach**: As you climb up, lift others. Guide junior product managers, sharing your experiences and insights.

5. **Continuous Learning**: The tech and product landscape is ever-evolving. Attend seminars, workshops, and courses to stay ahead.

The Challenges of Leadership

With great power comes greater responsibilities and challenges:

- **Balancing Strategy and Execution**: Leaders often miss diving deep into products. Ensure you don't lose touch with the product's core, even as you strategize.

- **Team Dynamics**: You're not just leading products but people. Each team member will have aspirations, strengths, and areas of improvement. Navigating this can be challenging.

- **Decision Making**: The stakes are higher. Your decisions will have broader impacts, and not all will be well-received.

A Tale of Transformation: Sarah's Journey

Sarah began as a product manager, responsible for one of its flagship apps. With her sharp acumen, she often foresaw market shifts and adapted the product accordingly. Recognizing her potential, the company provided her with opportunities to mentor new PMs, slowly increasing her engagement with executives.

Over time, she transitioned from not just managing her app but setting the strategic direction for all apps under the company's banner. She became the bridge between the C-suite's business goals and the product team's aspirations. With time, she evolved from being a manager of products to a leader of people, vision, and strategy.

Final Reflections

The journey from a product manager to a product leader isn't just about advancing in one's career but growing in one's understanding of products, markets, people, and oneself. It's about moving from executing visions to setting them, from managing backlogs to inspiring teams, and from meeting targets to setting them. Embrace the journey with open arms and a growth mindset!

40

Building and Mentoring Product Teams

Laying the Foundation: Crafting the Perfect Team

Success in product management is seldom an individual's achievement. More often, it is the result of a cohesive team working harmoniously towards a shared vision. As a product leader, your role extends beyond products and strategies to building and mentoring the teams that bring these products to life.

Steps to Build an Exceptional Product Team

1. **Identify Key Roles**: Understand the critical roles required for your product. This typically includes product managers, UX/UI designers, data analysts, and engineers. However, depending on the product, you may need more specialized roles.

2. **Hire for Skill and Culture Fit**: While expertise is essential, hiring someone aligned with the company's culture and values ensures smoother collaboration.

3. **Diverse Perspectives**: Building a team with varied backgrounds and experiences brings a richer set of perspectives to problem-solving.

4. **Clear Role Definitions**: Ensure every team member understands their responsibilities. This clarity reduces overlaps and gaps.

Mentoring: Shaping the Next Generation of Leaders

1. **One-on-One Sessions**: Spend quality time with each team member. Understand their aspirations, strengths, and areas they want to improve.

2. **Encourage Continuous Learning**: Promote a culture where team members are encouraged to upskill, attend workshops, or take courses relevant to their roles.

3. **Provide Constructive Feedback**: Be open and honest with your feedback, ensuring it's constructive and actionable.

4. **Celebrate Wins**: Acknowledge and celebrate small victories. This boosts morale and instills a sense of ownership and pride.

5. **Facilitate Peer Mentoring**: Encourage experienced team members to mentor newer members. This not only speeds up onboarding but also fosters a culture of knowledge sharing.

Challenges in Building and Mentoring

- **Scaling Teams**: As products grow, so do the teams. Ensuring communication remains clear and roles well-defined becomes challenging.

- **Conflict Resolution**: With diverse minds come diverse opinions. As a leader, mediating conflicts and ensuring the team remains aligned is crucial.

- **Ensuring Consistent Growth**: Mentoring isn't a one-time task. Continuously tracking team member growth and providing opportunities becomes pivotal.

A Story of Transformation: Alex's Ensemble

When Alex was appointed the lead product role, he inherited a small but competent team. Recognizing the potential, he embarked on a hiring spree, ensuring he brought in not just skill but diverse perspectives.

However, with growth came challenges. The team, once working seamlessly, began experiencing conflicts. Silos formed, affecting product delivery.

Recognizing the pitfalls, Alex initiated one-on-one sessions, understanding individual grievances, and aspirations. He also initiated team-building exercises, ensuring the team bonded outside work. Peer mentoring became a norm, with senior members guiding newer ones.

Months passed, and the changes became evident. The team, once fragmented, now operated as a single unit. Their first major product launch post this transformation was a resounding success, a testament to Alex's belief in the power of building and mentoring.

In Summation

Building a team is more than just hiring. It's about nurturing a group of individuals into a cohesive unit, aligned in vision and purpose. As a product leader, you're not just shaping products but also the individuals who bring these products to life. Embrace this role with empathy, vision, and commitment.

41

Managing Multiple Products

The Juggle of Multiple Hats: Embracing Complexity

The transition from managing a single product to multiple products can be akin to a solo performer becoming an orchestra conductor. The stage is bigger, instruments more varied, and the symphony—while richer—requires precise coordination. Let's explore the art and science of overseeing several products.

Strategies for Effective Multi-Product Management

1. **Portfolio Vision and Strategy**: Ensure that you have a clear vision for your product portfolio. Each product should have its purpose and desired outcome in the broader organizational goal.

2. **Resource Allocation**: Resources are finite. Whether it's time, budget, or manpower, understanding where to allocate more and where to pull back is crucial.

3. **Prioritization at Scale**: While prioritization within a single product is complex, doing it across products can be even trickier. Leveraging systematic approaches and prioritization frameworks can be invaluable.

4. **Dedicated Teams**: Whenever possible, have dedicated teams for each product. This avoids context-switching and ensures focus.

5. **Unified Communication Channels**: Ensure there's a clear communication channel that covers all products. Regular portfolio reviews can help in keeping everyone aligned.

Interdependencies and Synergies

1. **Shared Learnings**: Encourage teams to share insights and learnings across products. An improvement in one product can often be adapted to others.

2. **Identifying Cross-Selling Opportunities**: Look for opportunities where one product can enhance the value of another, leading to cross-promotion or bundling opportunities.

Challenges and Their Solutions

- **Dilution of Focus**: With multiple products, there's a risk of losing depth. Solution? Regular deep dives into each product to understand nuances and challenges.

- **Resource Conflicts**: Multiple products can vie for the same resources. Solution? An objective resource allocation framework that's communicated clearly to all teams.

- **Mixed Messaging**: Different products might send varied messages to the market. Solution? A unified brand voice and messaging guideline.

A Tale of Three Apps

Rebecca was at the helm of AppA when she was tasked with overseeing AppB and AppC. Initially, she tried managing all three with the same detail she did AppA. Burnout loomed large.

Taking a step back, she restructured her approach. She began with a portfolio vision, identifying where each app fit. Dedicated teams were set up, and she ensured a structured communication process was established, enabling her to get updates without micromanaging.

She also encouraged the teams to communicate amongst themselves, leading to AppA's successful feature being adapted into AppB. Resource clashes were handled by setting up a transparent allocation process, reducing conflicts.

In a year, not only did all three apps see growth, but Rebecca also found herself enjoying the process, turning potential chaos into harmonized success.

In Conclusion

Managing multiple products isn't merely about multiplying the effort of managing one. It requires a holistic view, understanding interdependencies, and embracing both the challenges and opportunities it brings. With the right strategies and mindset, it can be a rewarding journey of growth and learning.

42

Scaling Product Operations Efficiently

Introduction

Scaling product operations is much like steering a ship through uncharted waters. The open sea represents opportunities, but without the right compass, navigational charts, or crew, the journey can become perilous. For a Product Manager, scaling is more than just growing; it's about growing wisely and efficiently. The journey, while challenging, is immensely rewarding if navigated correctly.

1. Establishing a Clear Vision and Mission

Before scaling, clarity is crucial. The product vision and mission should be the North Star guiding all decisions. When operations expand, the foundational principles must remain consistent. This ensures that no matter how big the team or diverse the product line, everyone is aligned and moving in the same direction.

2. Implementing Robust Systems and Processes

With growth comes complexity. Manual processes that once worked may now be bottlenecks. It's essential to automate repetitive tasks and streamline workflows. Implementing agile methodologies, using project management tools, and integrating platforms can offer visibility and ensure everyone is on the same page.

3. Building a Cohesive Team Structure

As product operations scale, the team might need to grow or be restructured. It might be time to introduce roles like Product Operations Manager or even specialized product managers for distinct product lines. Regardless of the size, ensure the team fosters open communication, collaboration, and a culture of continuous learning.

4. Efficient Resource Allocation

Resource constraints can become evident during scaling. Efficiently allocating resources, be it manpower, budget, or tools, is paramount. Prioritization becomes critical. Tools and frameworks can aid in ensuring that the highest impact tasks are addressed first, maximizing ROI.

5. Continuous Feedback Loop

An expanding product operation means more user feedback, more data, and more insights. Incorporating a continuous feedback mechanism helps iterate on features, understand market shifts, and make necessary pivots. It's this feedback-driven approach that will keep the product relevant and user-centric.

6. Ensuring Quality at Scale

The temptation during rapid scaling might be to release more features quickly. However, quality should never be compromised. Implement rigorous testing, quality checks, and ensure the team understands the importance of maintaining the product's standard. A robust QA process becomes non-negotiable.

7. Training and Onboarding

With growth, new members will join the product family. Efficient onboarding processes ensure they align with the product vision quickly. Regular training sessions, workshops, and certifications can ensure the team's skills are always up-to-date.

8. Maintaining Flexibility

While processes and systems are crucial, maintaining a degree of flexibility is essential. The market is dynamic, user needs evolve, and technology advances rapidly. The product operations should be agile enough to adapt to these changes without causing significant disruptions.

Conclusion

Scaling product operations is a significant milestone, reflecting success and market validation. However, it's also a juncture where many challenges arise. With the right strategies, systems, and mindset, Product Managers can ensure that scaling is not just about growing bigger, but also about growing better.

43
Creating a Culture of Innovation

Introduction

Innovation is the lifeline of any thriving company. It's not just about revolutionary products or disruptive technologies; it's about fostering an environment where every individual feels empowered to think differently. For Product Managers, nurturing a culture of innovation can be the key to staying ahead in an ever-evolving marketplace.

1. The Power of the 'Why'

Before delving into strategies and tactics, teams need to understand the 'why' behind innovation. This means recognizing that innovation is not an end in itself but a means to solve real-world problems, delight customers, and ensure long-term business sustainability.

2. Encourage Curiosity

The best innovations often come from the most inquisitive minds. Encourage your team to ask questions, challenge the status quo, and think beyond the confines of their roles. Regular brainstorming sessions, where every idea is valued, can be a great starting point.

3. Diverse Teams, Diverse Ideas

Diversity fuels innovation. A team with varied backgrounds, experiences, and perspectives will inevitably view challenges differently and come up with a broader range of solutions. Cultivate a team environment where diversity is celebrated and leveraged.

4. Provide Safe Spaces for Failure

Innovation involves risks, and not every idea will succeed. However, fear of failure can stifle creativity. Create an environment where failure is seen as a learning opportunity, not a setback. Celebrate the effort and the learnings that come from it.

5. Invest in Continuous Learning

The world is evolving at breakneck speeds. Workshops, training sessions, and courses should be a regular feature, ensuring your team stays updated with the latest trends, tools, and technologies. Knowledge is the bedrock upon which innovation is built.

6. Recognize and Reward Innovation

Recognition goes a long way in reinforcing desired behaviors. When team members come up with innovative ideas or solutions, celebrate them. Whether through awards, shout-outs, or tangible rewards, let them know their innovative spirit is valued.

7. Allocate Time for Creative Thinking

In the hustle and bustle of daily tasks, creative thinking can take a backseat. Introduce practices like "Innovation Fridays" where team members spend a few hours solely brainstorming or working on side projects. Google's '20% time' policy, which led to products like Gmail, is a testament to this approach's power.

8. Open Channels of Communication

Innovation thrives in transparent environments. Open communication ensures that ideas aren't siloed within departments but can flow freely across the organization. Platforms or regular meetings where teams can share updates and insights can be immensely beneficial.

9. Collaborate with External Thinkers

Sometimes, an external perspective can provide fresh insights. Collaborate with industry experts, academicians, or even startups. These interactions can introduce new ways of thinking and spark innovative ideas.

Conclusion

Innovation isn't just about the next big product or feature. It's a mindset, a culture where every challenge is seen as an opportunity to think differently. As Product Managers, creating and nurturing this culture is one of the most profound legacies one can leave, ensuring the organization remains relevant, agile, and ever-evolving.

Part 10: Special Topics

44

The Role of Artificial Intelligence in Product Management

Introduction

In the digital age, Artificial Intelligence (AI) stands as a beacon of potential, especially within the realms of product management. From automated customer support to insightful analytics, AI is transforming the way products are conceived, designed, and optimized. Journey with us as we unravel the intricate tapestry of AI's influence on modern product management.

1. Unraveling Complex Data

The quantum of data available to product managers today is staggering. AI acts as a torchbearer, illuminating patterns and insights from this vast sea of information. Through Machine Learning algorithms, AI sifts through data, offering product managers actionable insights about user behavior, preferences, and pain points.

Snapshot: Amazon's AI-powered Forecasting Amazon leverages AI to predict what products users might buy next, ensuring optimal stock levels and tailoring marketing strategies accordingly.

2. Proactive Product Evolution

Gone are the days of reacting to market changes. With AI, product managers can predict them. Predictive analytics, fueled by AI, can gauge future trends, allowing managers to evolve products proactively, staying ahead of the competition.

3. A Personal Touch at Scale

Personalization isn't new. But with AI, personalization is elevated. Consider chatbots that handle myriad customer queries simultaneously or recommendation systems that cater to individual tastes.

Snapshot: *YouTube's* *Algorithm* YouTube's recommendation engine uses AI to analyze watch histories and user behaviors, curating a personalized video playlist for each user, enhancing engagement.

4. Streamlining Repetitive Chores

Routine tasks can bog down the creative spirit. AI steps in as a savior, automating mundane tasks like data aggregation, basic analytics, or even customer feedback collection, giving product managers more time for strategic planning.

5. AI-Driven Prototyping

Imagine creating a prototype that's already user-tested. AI can simulate user interactions, offering insights into potential challenges and acceptance rates, even before a product sees the light of day.

6. Revolutionizing Product Testing

Beyond traditional testing, AI can simulate diverse user environments and behaviors. By creating thousands of virtual user scenarios, AI ensures products are robust and user-centric.

7. AI's Double-Edged Sword: Ethics

While AI promises a world of opportunities, it brings along a bundle of ethical concerns. Transparency in AI processes, data privacy, and avoiding inherent biases become paramount for product managers.

Snapshot: Controversies Around AI Job Screening Tools
Several companies adopted AI-driven job screening tools, only to face backlash for potential biases. It emphasized the need for ethical AI use.

Conclusion

Artificial Intelligence, in its essence, is reshaping the product management domain. As it seamlessly intertwines with various product stages, its potential seems boundless. However, with great power comes great responsibility. Product managers must harmoniously blend AI's prowess with ethical considerations, ensuring they create products that are not just smart but also resonate with human values.

<h1 style="text-align:center">45</h1>

Navigating Regulatory and Compliance Issues

Introduction

Regulatory compliance isn't merely a checkbox to tick off—it's an integral facet of building and managing products. Especially for product managers in sensitive sectors like healthcare, finance, and data-intensive industries, understanding the landscape of regulations and compliance becomes paramount. Dive deep as we explore the maze of regulatory compliance and its significance in product management.

1. Understanding Why Regulations Matter

At the heart of regulations lie consumer protection, ethical standards, and market integrity. By ensuring products comply with established standards, product managers not only avoid legal pitfalls but also fortify consumer trust.

Snapshot: The General Data Protection Regulation (GDPR) Effect When the European Union rolled out GDPR, companies had to revamp their data handling practices, impacting product features, data storage, and user interfaces.

2. Building a Compliance-Conscious Team

Product development isn't a solo act. From developers to marketers, ensuring every team member understands the regulatory framework is essential. Regular training sessions, workshops, and updates can help keep the team aligned.

3. Integrating Compliance into Product Design

It's more cost-effective to build compliance into the product from the start than to retrofit it later. Product managers should involve legal and compliance experts during the design and prototyping phases.

4. Continuous Monitoring & Adaptation

Regulations evolve, and so should products. Continuous monitoring ensures that products remain compliant. Any regulatory change should trigger a product review to ascertain compliance.

5. Document, Document, Document

Documentation isn't glamorous, but it's crucial. Maintaining comprehensive records of product decisions, design changes, and compliance checks can be invaluable during audits or regulatory inspections.

Snapshot: Fintech and Regulatory Scrutiny
Many fintech startups maintain rigorous documentation as they are often under regulatory scrutiny, ensuring they can justify every product choice in line with financial regulations.

6. Leveraging Technology for Compliance

Use technology as an ally. Compliance management tools can automatically flag non-compliance, maintain records, or even adapt product features based on regulatory updates.

7. Preparing for Global Complexities

For products with a global footprint, navigating the regulatory landscape becomes trickier. Each market may have its own set of rules. It's essential to localize not just language but also compliance.

8. The Human Element: Ethics Beyond Compliance

Beyond regulations lies the broader realm of ethics. Product managers should foster an environment where ethical considerations are discussed, and the right decisions are made, even when regulations are silent.

Conclusion

Regulatory and compliance issues might seem daunting, but they are surmountable. With a proactive approach, thorough understanding, and a commitment to doing right by the users, product managers can turn compliance from a challenge into an opportunity for building better, safer, and more trustworthy products.

46
The Rise of Remote Product Management

Introduction

The rise of remote work isn't just a fleeting trend but a profound shift in how organizations operate. Particularly for product managers, who once believed in the sanctity of whiteboard brainstorming and in-person user interviews, this transition challenges traditional approaches. Let's traverse the evolution and best practices of remote product management.

A World Turned Upside Down: Pandemic as the Catalyst

The seeds for remote work were sown long before the global events like the 2020 pandemic. The COVID-19 pandemic accelerated the transition, converting skeptics overnight. Firms that had never considered remote work as viable were suddenly compelled to embrace it.

Case Study: XYZ Corp's Swift Transition to Remote Product Management

Background: XYZ Corp, a mid-sized tech company, had always been an in-office operation. The pandemic left them no choice but to adapt rapidly.

Challenge: Transitioning to remote product management while ensuring that the quality of collaboration, product development, and user research didn't decline.

Action:

- **Tool Adoption**: XYZ integrated Teams for team communication, and SharePoint for documentation.

- **Team Training**: Conducted workshops on remote work best practices, ensuring every team member was equipped for the shift.

Result: After an initial adaptation period, XYZ Corp found their product teams were as efficient remotely as they were in the office. Surprisingly, some teams reported improved efficiency and job satisfaction.

Sustaining Team Dynamics and Culture

Remote teams needed to invest more in relationship-building:

- **Virtual Coffee Breaks**: Casual video chats to replace water-cooler talk.

- **Online Team-building**: Games, quizzes, and shared movie nights fostered camaraderie.

- **Feedback Mechanisms**: Regularly soliciting feedback on the remote working experience to continually adapt and improve.

The Unintended Benefits of Remote Product Management

- **Global Talent Acquisition**: Geographic limitations disappeared, expanding the talent pool.

- **Flexibility and Diversity**: Different time zones meant longer overall team availability. Plus, remote work provided inclusivity for those with physical disabilities or other challenges.

The Future: Hybrid Models and Beyond

Some organizations, having tasted the benefits of remote product management, are considering hybrid models — a blend of in-person and remote. This offers teams flexibility while preserving the advantages of face-to-face interactions when necessary.

Conclusion

The rise of remote product management is a testament to the adaptability of industries and professionals. With the right tools, strategies, and mindset, product teams worldwide have turned challenges into growth opportunities.

47

Leveraging Customer Co-Creation for Product Innovation

In the ever-evolving landscape of product management, staying attuned to customer needs and preferences is paramount. One innovative approach that has emerged is Customer Co-Creation, a collaborative effort between the organization and its customers to create value. This is a shift from the traditional model where companies create value and deliver it to customers. Instead, co-creation engages customers directly in the innovation process, ensuring that the final product resonates with the end-users.

Benefits of Customer Co-Creation:

1. **Deeper Customer Understanding**: By engaging customers in the creation process, product managers gain deeper insights into their needs, preferences, and pain points, which can lead to more customer-centric solutions.

2. **Enhanced Innovation**: Co-creation brings diverse perspectives to the table, fostering a culture of innovation. The blend of ideas from both customers and the internal team can lead to the development of unique solutions.

3. **Increased Customer Loyalty and Satisfaction**: Customers who are involved in the co-creation process are likely to feel a sense of ownership and connection to the product, resulting in higher satisfaction and loyalty.

Implementing Customer Co-Creation:

1. **Identify and Select Co-Creation Participants**: Choose a diverse group of customers to participate in the co-creation process. Ensure a mix of demographics to gain a wide range of perspectives.

2. **Establish Clear Objectives and Guidelines**: Set clear goals for the co-creation process, and ensure all participants understand the guidelines and expected outcomes.

3. **Create a Collaborative Environment**: Foster a culture of openness where participants feel comfortable sharing their ideas. Utilize collaborative tools and platforms to facilitate communication and idea sharing.

4. **Iterate and Refine Based on Feedback**: Continuously gather feedback from the co-creation participants and iterate on the product accordingly. This iterative process is crucial for refining the product to meet customer needs.

Case Study:

1. **LEGO Ideas**: LEGO has successfully implemented a customer co-creation platform called LEGO Ideas. Here, LEGO enthusiasts submit their designs, and the community votes on their favorites. Winning designs are turned into official LEGO sets, and creators are rewarded with a share of the sales.

2. **Starbucks' My Starbucks Idea**: Starbucks launched a platform where customers could share their ideas for improving products and services. This initiative led to the creation of many new offerings, including the popular Pumpkin Spice Latte.

3. **Unilever's Open Innovation**: Unilever has an open innovation platform inviting customers, suppliers, and independent inventors to submit ideas for new technologies or solutions. This has accelerated their innovation process, bringing fresh perspectives and solutions to the company.

In conclusion, customer co-creation is a powerful tool for product innovation, bringing customers closer to the product and fostering a culture of continuous improvement and innovation. Through effective implementation and real-world examples, it's evident that embracing co-creation can lead to remarkable product advancements and enhanced customer satisfaction.

48

Case Study: Turning Around a Failing Product

Introduction

In the intricate world of semiconductors, product precision and performance are paramount. The industry, with its rapid advancements and high stakes, offers little room for error. This case study uncovers the tale of a semiconductor company ChipMakers., which salvaged a potential disaster and repositioned a failing product as a market leader.

Background: ChipMakers, a semiconductor company, was ready to launch QuantumX, a chip designed for the next generation of smartphones. Initial projections anticipated high demand, but the reality post-launch was starkly different. Returns were skyrocketing, and negative reviews from major tech firms were flowing in.

Diagnosing the Problem

1. **Technical Assessment**: An internal review revealed that QuantumX had overheating issues when subjected to multitasking, a crucial feature for smartphones.

2. **Market Analysis**: The competition had released chips with similar performance metrics but without the associated heating issues.

3. **Feedback Loop**: Major tech companies reported concerns about the chip's longevity and potential harm to other smartphone components due to overheating.

Strategizing the Revival

1. Rapid Response Team:

- ChipMakers formed a cross-functional team of engineers, product managers, and quality assurance specialists to delve deep into the issue.

2. Technical Refinement:

- After rigorous testing, the team identified design flaws in the chip architecture. They initiated a redesign to optimize power consumption and reduce heat.

3. Transparent Communication:

- ChipMakers engaged with their B2B clients, explaining the steps they were taking and offering discounts on future bulk orders as a goodwill gesture.

4. R&D Investments:

- Realizing that in-depth research was pivotal, ChipMakers invested in advanced testing facilities to prevent such mishaps in the future.

The Recovery: QuantumX's Redemption

The relaunch of QuantumX, post-refinements, was met with acclaim. Previous clients appreciated the company's proactive approach, and QuantumX began to feature in flagship smartphone models. Within a year, the chip's market share increased by 30%.

Key Takeaways:

1. **Swift Problem Addressal**: Quick recognition of issues and their addressal can mitigate long-term damage.

2. **Stakeholder Communication is Vital**: Being transparent and open about product flaws with stakeholders can help in damage control and trust retention.

3. **R&D is a Safety Net**: Investing in R&D ensures that potential product issues can be identified and rectified during the developmental phase.

Conclusion

ChipMakers' experience with QuantumX serves as a testament to the importance of timely interventions, stakeholder communication, and the role of R&D in the semiconductor industry. Mistakes can occur, even in precision industries, but a company's response strategy is what shapes its reputation and future success.

Part 11: Preparing for the Future
49
Predicting and Shaping Future Trends

Introduction

As a Product Manager, one's role isn't confined to managing existing products; it's about foreseeing the future, understanding where markets are heading, and preparing products to fit within that landscape. In a constantly evolving marketplace, staying ahead of trends is crucial.

1. The Role of Data in Predicting Trends

- **Historical Analysis**: Historical sales, usage, and feedback data can provide insights into patterns and help predict future shifts.

- **Real-time Analytics**: Tools that provide real-time data can help PMs adapt quickly to emerging trends.

2. Engaging Directly with Users

- **Feedback Systems**: Always maintain a clear channel for users to express their needs, desires, and frustrations.

- **Consumer Forums**: Organize or participate in forums where consumers discuss products, which can reveal unmet needs and future directions.

3. Monitoring Global Markets

The world is interconnected, and trends often emerge globally before becoming local:

- **Cross-border Studies**: Understand user behavior across different markets.

- **Adopt & Adapt Strategy**: Emulate successful strategies from one market, and customize them for another.

4. Collaborative Approach to Trendspotting

- **Idea-sharing Platforms**: Internal platforms where teams can share observations and insights can be a rich source for trend predictions.

- **Engaging with Industry Think Tanks**: This provides an external perspective on where the industry is headed.

5. The Tech Impact

- **Emerging Technologies**: Stay informed about advancements in tech that could impact or disrupt your product.

- **Invest in R&D**: Dedicate resources to experiment with new technologies to prepare for future integration.

6. Proactive Trendsetting

Sometimes, predicting trends is not enough; PMs can also be trendsetters.

- **Pilot Projects**: Test out potential future trends on a smaller scale to gauge their viability.

- **Market Education**: Create educational content around new trends or uses of your product to guide the market in the desired direction.

Case Study: The Rise of Plant-based Meat Alternatives

The shift towards more sustainable and health-conscious eating habits was being observed globally. A few companies saw the potential of this emerging trend early on. Beyond Meat, a company producing plant-based meat substitutes, is a prime example.

Beyond Meat's Product Managers understood the importance of not just creating a plant-based alternative but making it taste and feel like real meat. Their focus was on the entire experience. They observed several trends:

1. A rise in veganism and vegetarianism.

2. Increased focus on sustainable agricultural practices.

3. Consumer concern regarding animal welfare.

By aligning their product development with these trends, Beyond Meat was not only ahead of the curve but also played a role in shaping the trend itself. Their success led to a surge in similar products entering the market, reinforcing the trend they had predicted and nurtured.

Conclusion

The ability to predict and shape trends is a combination of vigilant observation, data interpretation, understanding user behavior, and sometimes, a touch of intuition. While predicting the future with absolute certainty is impossible, the tools and strategies mentioned can equip a Product Manager to be more prepared and possibly even be a trendsetter.

50

Evaluating and Integrating Emerging Business Models

In a landscape where innovation is the cornerstone of sustainability and growth, the emergence of novel business models is a commonplace yet disruptive force. These models can alter the status quo, challenging established enterprises and making adaptability a critical asset. As a product manager, understanding, evaluating, and integrating these emerging business models into your strategies can not only cushion against unforeseen market shifts but can also position your product for future success.

Understanding Emerging Business Models

The first step in this endeavor is to understand what constitutes an emerging business model. These models often arise from technological advancements, changes in consumer preferences, or shifts in regulatory landscapes. They may redefine how value is created, delivered, and captured within an industry. Notable examples from the past include the shift from traditional retail to e-commerce, the advent of subscription-based services, and the rise of the gig economy.

Evaluating New Business Models

Evaluating new business models requires a nuanced approach. It encompasses a thorough analysis of the model's viability, scalability, and the value proposition it offers. Key considerations should include:

1. **Market Demand:** Assessing whether there is a substantial market demand for the value proposition the new business model offers.

2. **Competitive Advantage:** Determining if the model provides a sustainable competitive advantage.

3. **Alignment with Core Competencies:** Checking the alignment of the model with the existing core competencies of your organization.

4. **Financial Viability:** Analyzing the financial implications including the revenue model, cost structure, and profitability potential.

Integration Strategies

Once an emerging business model is deemed viable, the next phase is integration. This involves aligning the new model with the existing operations, culture, and strategic goals of your organization. Key steps in this phase could include:

1. **Pilot Testing:** Before a full-scale integration, conduct pilot tests to gauge the model's impact and identify potential roadblocks.

2. **Cross-functional Collaboration:** Engage cross-functional teams to ensure smooth integration and to leverage diverse insights.

3. **Continuous Monitoring and Adjustment:** Post-integration, continuously monitor the performance of the new model and be ready to make adjustments as necessary.

Preparing for Disruption

The ability to anticipate, evaluate, and integrate new business models is a hallmark of a forward-thinking product manager. It prepares the organization to better handle the disruptions and take advantage of the opportunities these new models present.

Moreover, promoting a culture of openness and continuous learning among your team can foster an environment conducive to adapting to new business models. Encouraging your team to stay informed about industry shifts and emerging trends can further bolster your product's position in a future shaped by evolving business models.

Conclusion

The integration of emerging business models is not a one-size-fits-all approach but a nuanced, iterative process. It demands a keen understanding of the market dynamics, a thorough evaluation of the new model, and a strategic approach to integration. By staying proactive in this domain, product managers can not only safeguard their products against disruptive forces but also seize new avenues of growth and innovation.

51

Preparing for Unexpected Market Shifts

Introduction

The dynamism of the modern marketplace means unpredictability. Product managers are often caught in the maelstrom of unforeseen shifts that can redefine an entire industry overnight. Whether catalyzed by groundbreaking technologies, global socio-economic changes, or black swan events, navigating these shifts successfully is pivotal.

Understanding Market Volatility

Before one can prepare, one must understand. Market shifts are not always chaotic; they often have underlying triggers. Sometimes it's a technological leap, at other times a socio-cultural movement or a global incident. For instance, the rise of smartphones transformed many industries, while the COVID-19 pandemic reshaped the way businesses operate.

Spotting the Early Signs

The key to preparedness is observation. Regularly monitor:

1. **Industry News:** Stay updated with industry-specific news and broader technological and socio-cultural trends.

2. **Consumer Behavior:** Track behavioral changes in your user base and the broader market.

3. **Competitor Movement:** Competitor adaptations can be early signals of a shift.

Strategizing for Shocks

Once you're attuned to the signs, the next step is to build a responsive strategy:

1. **Flexibility:** Keep plans adaptable. Understand that roadmaps might need rapid revisions.

2. **Diversification:** Spread your bets. Avoid over-reliance on a single product or market segment.

3. **Scenario Planning:** Regularly envision potential market changes and craft tentative strategies.

Case Study: Blockbuster vs. Netflix

Blockbuster, the video rental giant, was an undeniable market leader in the 1990s. However, they failed to spot the signs of a shift towards digital streaming and the demand for home entertainment. Netflix, starting as a DVD-by-mail service, quickly adapted to the online streaming model.

While Blockbuster was burdened by its physical stores and late fees, Netflix invested in content and technology. By the time Blockbuster attempted to compete in the digital space, it was too late. Netflix had captured the market, and Blockbuster filed for bankruptcy in 2010.

Lesson: The inability to anticipate and adapt to market shifts can be fatal, even for market leaders.

Cultivating a Resilient Team

A nimble team can make all the difference:

1. **Continuous Learning:** Encourage your team to regularly update their skills.

2. **Open Communication Channels:** Foster an environment where insights and observations are openly shared.

3. **Encourage Innovation:** Allow team members to experiment and come up with adaptive strategies.

Financial and Operational Preparedness

Ensure the organization is ready to handle shocks:

1. **Financial Cushioning:** Have reserves for sudden R&D needs or to cushion a downturn.

2. **Operational Scalability:** Ensure that operations can be scaled up or down swiftly based on requirements.

Conclusion

Unexpected market shifts are a challenge, but with the right strategies, they can also be opportunities. By maintaining a pulse on the market, being agile, and fostering a resilient team culture, product managers can not only navigate these shifts but also emerge stronger. The future belongs to those who are prepared.

52

Building Sustainable and Environmentally Friendly Products

Introduction

In an age where environmental concerns take center stage, consumers are increasingly inclined towards sustainable products. Product managers, therefore, have a renewed responsibility to not just meet market demands but also ensure that their products tread lightly on our planet.

Understanding Sustainable Product Development

At its core, sustainable product development seeks to create products that have a minimal negative impact on the environment while delivering maximum value to the consumer. This process involves considering every stage of the product lifecycle, from sourcing raw materials to end-of-life disposal.

The Importance of Eco-Friendly Products

1. **Consumer Demand:** A growing section of consumers prefer products that are environmentally friendly.

2. **Regulatory Compliance:** Many countries are imposing stricter environmental regulations.

3. **Cost-Efficiency:** Sustainable products often lead to savings in the long run due to waste reduction and efficient use of resources.

4. **Brand Reputation:** Companies that prioritize sustainability often enjoy a more positive brand image.

Key Considerations in Building Sustainable Products

1. **Material Sourcing:** Opt for renewable, recyclable, or biodegradable materials.

2. **Energy Efficiency:** Ensure the product consumes minimal energy during production and usage.

3. **Waste Management:** Adopt processes that reduce waste and promote recycling.

4. **Supply Chain:** Collaborate with suppliers and partners who also prioritize sustainability.

Case Study: Patagonia's Sustainable Approach

Outdoor clothing brand Patagonia has long been a beacon for sustainable product management. Their commitment is evident in initiatives such as the "Worn Wear" program, where customers are encouraged to buy used Patagonia items or trade in their old ones.

Furthermore, Patagonia invests heavily in R&D to find eco-friendly materials for their products. Their Yulex wetsuits, for instance, use natural rubber instead of neoprene, reducing CO_2 emissions during production by up to 80%.

Lesson: Sustainability can be a unique selling point, fostering brand loyalty and attracting a conscious consumer base.

Challenges in Sustainable Product Management

1. **Initial Costs:** Eco-friendly materials and processes can be more expensive initially.

2. **Consumer Education:** Customers might need to be educated about the benefits of a sustainable product, especially if it comes at a premium.

3. **Balancing Act:** Striking the right balance between sustainability, product quality, and affordability can be challenging.

Engaging Stakeholders in the Sustainable Journey

1. **Internal Training:** Educate your team about the importance and methods of sustainable product development.

2. **Customer Feedback:** Engage with consumers to understand their sustainability preferences and to educate them about your efforts.

3. **Collaboration:** Partner with environmental NGOs or consultants to improve your sustainability practices.

Conclusion

Building sustainable and environmentally friendly products is no longer a niche approach but a necessity in today's market landscape. While the journey towards complete sustainability is complex, it is rewarding both in terms of brand reputation and long-term profitability. Product managers who prioritize eco-friendliness will not only contribute to a healthier planet but will also be better equipped to meet the demands of the modern, conscious consumer.

53

The Role of Product Managers in a Post-COVID World

Introduction

The COVID-19 pandemic was an unprecedented event that reshaped industries, consumer behaviors, and global markets. In this evolving landscape, product managers faced new challenges and opportunities, requiring them to redefine their roles and strategies. Navigating the post-COVID world calls for adaptability, foresight, and an understanding of the "new normal."

Understanding the Post-COVID Landscape

COVID-19 drastically changed the way businesses operate and consumers behave. Remote work became the norm, e-commerce surged, and there was a heightened focus on digital experiences. Additionally, consumer values shifted towards health, safety, and sustainability. Product managers need to comprehend these shifts and adapt their products accordingly.

Key Changes for Product Managers

1. **Digital Transformation:** With the surge in online activity, product managers need to prioritize digital solutions, ensuring seamless user experiences.

2. **Agility and Flexibility:** Rapidly changing regulations and market dynamics demand agile product development and adaptability.

3. **Consumer-Centric Approach:** Understanding the new consumer needs, especially around safety and reliability, became paramount.

4. **Sustainability and Ethics:** The pandemic highlighted the importance of sustainability and ethical considerations in product development.

Case Study: Zoom's Rise in the Pandemic

When the pandemic forced the world indoors, there was an immediate need for reliable video conferencing tools. Zoom, although already a popular tool, rose to the challenge by rapidly enhancing its capacity, improving security measures, and introducing features to cater to the exploding demand from businesses, educators, and casual users alike.

Lesson: Zoom's success can be attributed to its quick adaptability, understanding of the evolving user needs, and effective product management.

Embracing Remote Product Management

1. **Collaborative Tools:** Product managers need to be proficient with tools that facilitate remote collaboration, from design to development.

2. **Effective Communication:** Clear communication becomes even more essential in a remote setup to ensure alignment and clarity.

3. **Building Trust:** Without face-to-face interactions, building trust within teams and with stakeholders is crucial.

Anticipating Future Disruptions

While the pandemic was a rare event, it underscored the need for product managers to be prepared for unforeseen disruptions. Scenario planning, keeping abreast of global trends, and fostering a culture of continuous learning can be pivotal.

Conclusion

The post-COVID world presented a unique set of challenges and opportunities for product managers. While the immediate crisis demanded swift actions and adaptability, the long-term implications require product managers to be visionary, ethical, and always aligned with the evolving needs of consumers. Embracing change, leveraging technology, and keeping the consumer at the heart of decisions will be the cornerstones for product managers navigating the post-COVID landscape.

54

Adapting to Emerging Technologies and Platforms

Introduction

The rapid advancement of technology and the emergence of new platforms present both challenges and opportunities for product managers. Keeping up with these changes is essential, as failing to adapt can lead to obsolescence, while timely adaptation can open doors to new avenues of growth.

Understanding Emerging Technologies and Platforms

Emerging technologies, such as Artificial Intelligence, blockchain, or quantum computing, often bring paradigm shifts in how industries operate. Platforms, on the other hand, refer to the digital or physical spaces where products are consumed, like VR platforms, voice-activated platforms, or new social media channels. As a product manager, being able to discern which of these trends will have staying power is crucial.

Key Considerations for Adaptation

1. **Market Relevance:** Will the technology or platform cater to a significant portion of your target audience or open up new segments?

2. **User Experience Enhancement:** Can the new technology or platform enhance the overall user experience of your product?

3. **Operational Viability:** What are the costs and challenges associated with integrating this technology?

4. **Strategic Alignment:** Does adopting the technology or platform align with your product's long-term goals?

Case Study: Snapchat's Adaptation to Augmented Reality (AR)

Snapchat, initially a simple photo-sharing app, identified the potential of AR early on. They introduced AR lenses that allowed users to overlay digital elements onto the real world through their camera. This adaptation not only enhanced user engagement but also opened up new monetization channels through branded lenses.

Lesson: Snapchat's success with AR underscores the importance of recognizing promising technologies and integrating them seamlessly to enhance user value.

Strategies for Effective Adaptation

1. **Continuous Learning:** Encourage a culture where teams are always updated about the latest tech trends through workshops, webinars, or courses.

2. **Collaboration with Experts:** Partner with tech experts or consultants to better understand the implications and applications of a technology.

3. **Pilot Testing:** Before a full-scale integration, test the technology on a smaller scale to gauge its efficacy and gather user feedback.

4. **Feedback Loops:** Post-integration, continuously gather feedback to refine and optimize the incorporation of the technology or platform.

Anticipating the Impacts of Technological Disruptions

Emerging technologies can disrupt industries overnight. As a product manager, it's crucial to always have a forward-looking vision, anticipating possible technological disruptions and preparing strategies to adapt or pivot as needed.

Conclusion

In the fast-paced world of technological advancements and emerging platforms, adaptability is key. For product managers, this means staying informed, being discerning about which trends to follow, and ensuring that the adoption of new technologies adds tangible value to the product and its users. Embracing this proactive approach ensures that products remain relevant, competitive, and equipped to serve the ever-evolving needs of the market.

Conclusion

55

The Ever-Evolving Role of the Product Manager

As the curtains draw on this enriching journey through the myriad facets of product management, it's imperative to pause and reflect on the fluid nature of the Product Manager's (PM) role. In a world where change is the only constant, a PM's role is akin to a river, ceaselessly flowing and adapting to the contours of the landscape it traverses.

1. **Voyage of Discovery:**

    - Embarking on a career in product management is akin to setting sail on a voyage of perpetual discovery. With each day bringing forth new challenges and learnings, the realm of product management is as exhilarating as it is enlightening.

2. **The Technological Tango:**

    - The dance with technology is a core aspect of a PM's journey. As technology gallops ahead with relentless vigor, a PM must match its pace with grace, understanding, and applying the evolving tech trends to keep the product relevant and competitive.

3. **Market Maven:**

    - A PM is a market maven, with an uncanny ability to sense the market pulse, adapting the product strategy like a chameleon to the colors of the market. This agility in responding to market dynamics keeps a product vibrant and in demand.

4. **Customer's Compass:**

    - A PM's North Star is the voice of the customer. As customer preferences evolve, so must the product. Staying attuned to the customer's voice, understanding their changing needs, and weaving those insights into the product is the mark of a successful PM.

5. **Collaboration Conductor:**

    - Orchestrating collaboration across a symphony of cross-functional teams is an art and science that a PM perfects over time. Ensuring a harmonious melody of teamwork towards a unified vision is crucial for the product's success.

6. **Ethical Evangelist:**

    - In a world burgeoning with data, a PM is an ethical evangelist ensuring the sanctity of user privacy and ethical practices in product development and data handling.

7. **Learning Luminary:**

    - The flame of curiosity and the thirst for learning is what keeps a PM's prowess sharp in the face of change. Embrace a culture of continuous learning, be it through books, courses, or mentorship, to stay ahead in the game.

8. **Innovation Incubator:**

    - Nurturing a culture of innovation is a vital part of a PM's role. Encouraging the team to think outside the box, to fail fast, learn faster, and to continuously iterate towards excellence, breeds a fertile ground for groundbreaking products.

9. **Global Gaze:**

- A PM today needs to have a global gaze, understanding the nuanced needs of diverse markets and cultures to create products that resonate across borders.

10. **Future Forward:**

    - Lastly, a PM is a futurist, always looking ahead, anticipating the uncharted waters, and preparing the ship to navigate through them with foresight and resilience.

In summation, being a Product Manager is a role replete with endless growth, continuous adaptation, and the joy of seeing one's efforts translate into products that touch lives. As you step into the future, may your passion for product management be the wind in your sails, propelling you towards uncharted horizons with a heart full of curiosity and a mind sharpened by the ever-evolving landscape of product management.

About the Author

Jianchun Xu stands out as a seasoned veteran in the realm of product management, celebrated for his innovative approach to new market entries and strategic product development. With a strong foundation in technical expertise coupled with outstanding managerial skills, he has consistently fostered successful business models and promoted product excellence throughout his career.

His experience in product management and marketing, particularly in the areas of semiconductor devices and power electronics, has positioned him as a key player in the industry. Having immersed himself in diverse cultures and work environments across Canada and Asia, Jianchun possesses a deep understanding of various market dynamics, allowing him to navigate complex business landscapes with ease. His academic background includes earning two Master's degrees in Electrical Engineering, from prestigious universities in Canada and China.

Characterized by his leadership, communication acumen, and strategic thinking, Jianchun excels in bringing together strategy, resources, and results. He is also a passionate advocate for continuous learning and professional development, which is reflected in his decision to author "55 Ways to Help You Be a Good Product Manager." In this comprehensive guide, Jianchun shares not just strategies and methodologies but also the wisdom and insights gleaned from a rich and diverse career.

This book is a heartfelt offering from Jianchun, reflecting his genuine passion for the field of product management. He humbly shares resources and insights, aspiring to assist others on their professional paths. Jianchun's deep-seated desire to contribute to the growth of emerging product leaders shines through in his thoughtful writing, as he seeks to gently guide and support the next wave of talent in navigating the complexities of product management.